# *Tinnitus*

## Related Titles

### The Psychological Management of Chronic Tinnitus:
### A Cognitive-Behavioral Approach
Jane L. Henry and Peter H. Wilson
ISBN: 0-205-31365-5

### Mechanisms of Tinnitus
Jack A. Vernon and Aage R. Moller
ISBN: 0-205-14083-1

### Tinnitus: Questions and Answers
Jack A. Vernon and Barbara Tabachnick Sanders
ISBN: 0-205-32685-4

### Tinnitus: Treatment and Relief
Jack A. Vernon
ISBN: 0-205-18269-0

For more information or to purchase a book, please call 1-800-278-3525.

# *Tinnitus*

## *A Self-Management Guide for the Ringing in Your Ears*

### Jane L. Henry

*University of New South Wales*

### Peter H. Wilson

*Southern Cross University*

### *Allyn and Bacon*

*Boston* • *London* • *Toronto* • *Sydney* • *Tokyo* • *Singapore*

*To Olwen and Paul—J. L. H.*

*To Louise, Michelle, and John—P. H. W.*

**Executive editor and publisher:** *Stephen D. Dragin*
**Editorial assistant:** *Barbara Strickland*
**Manufacturing buyer:** *Chris Marson*
**Marketing manager:** *Stephen Smith*
**Cover designer:** *Suzanne Harbison*
**Production coordinator:** *Pat Torelli Publishing Services*
**Editorial-production service:** *TKM Productions*
**Electronic composition:** *TKM Productions*

Copyright © 2002 by Allyn & Bacon
A Pearson Education Company
75 Arlington Street
Boston, MA 02116

Internet: www.ablongman.com

**Library of Congress Cataloging-in-Publication Data**

Henry, Jane L.
 Tinnitus : a self-management guide for the ringing in your ears / Jane L. Henry, Peter H. Wilson
  p. cm.
 Includes index.
 ISBN 0-205-31537-2
  1. Tinnitus. 2. Tinnitus--Treatment. 3. Tinnitus--Patients--Rehabilitation. 4. Self-care, Health. I. Wilson, Peter H.

 RF293.8 . H463 2001
 617.8--dc21                                                          2001016117

Printed in the United States of America

10  9  8  7  6  5  4  3  2  1     RRD-VA     05  04  03  02  01

**Permission credit:** Various quotations throughout this book are from Jane L. Henry and Peter H. Wilson, *Psychological Management of Tinnitus: A Cognitive-Behavioral Approach* (Boston: Allyn and Bacon, 2001). Reprinted by permission.

# Contents

# *Preface*

Imagine what it is like to be constantly aware of a high-pitched whistle that arises from within your ears or head and does not seem to be reduced by anything that you do—or something that sounds like a howling windstorm, a swarm of insects, a thumping machine. This is the experience of millions of people in the world who have a problem that is commonly called "ringing in the ears." This problem, or *tinnitus,* as it is more correctly called, is the subject of this book. Tinnitus affects up to 17 percent of people of all ages, backgrounds, and cultures. It has been historically reported for as long as there has been records of human activity. It is often, although not always, associated with other hearing problems, such as hearing impairment and sensitivity to noise. For many people, tinnitus is a significant cause of distress, often resulting in feelings of depression, anxiety, suicidal ideation, irritability, and frustration. Many individuals say that the worst problem they experience related to tinnitus is getting to sleep, because the tinnitus seems to be louder when there is little background noise. Tinnitus can also lead to significant disruptions to work, leisure, and everyday social activities. Only a small proportion of people respond to current medical and audiological treatments.

Many readers of this book who experience tinnitus are familiar with these difficulties and are seeking information regarding what to do about your tinnitus. You will be glad to know that this book is written primarily for you! Other readers may want to know more about this condition so that you can better understand what your relatives or friends with tinnitus are going through. Professionals who work in this area may also find this book valuable by gaining some useful insights and ideas about ways to advise people with tinnitus. In addition, there are always readers of any book who are just curious—who simply want to learn about tinnitus. We hope that you will find that this book opens up a world that is perhaps unknown to you. It may even give you some ideas about how to deal with similar problems, such as pain or other chronic medical difficulties. Many of the suggestions made in this book may be applicable to unpleasant or annoying situations in your own life.

In the absence of any well-established, universal cure, many people with tinnitus are told that they will need to "learn to live with the problem." Unfortunately, this advice is rarely backed up with any specific suggestions about *how* to learn to live with it. This task may seem almost impossible to someone who is experiencing a loud, constant, irritating noise from which he or she cannot escape and that nobody seems to understand. The aim of this book is to provide a comprehensive self-help guide for people with tinnitus. You will be provided with specific instructions in a range of techniques that will equip you with a variety of self-control skills so that you can effectively learn to live with your tinnitus.

The techniques described in this book cover methods that have been developed in recent years to help people to manage their tinnitus. These methods are generally referred to as cognitive-behavioral therapy, or CBT. There is now a growing body of scientific research that provides evidence for the efficacy of CBT in the management of tinnitus. The aim of these approaches to tinnitus is to help reduce the negative impact of tinnitus on your life and to lead to a state in which the tinnitus will be perceived to be less of a problem. In time, you may simply not notice the tinnitus as much, or you may be less bothered by it when you do notice it because you will have learned how to manage the problems caused by the tinnitus.

This book is written by professionals who have extensive clinical and research experience in the development, implementation, and evaluation of approaches to tinnitus. It is based on contemporary psychological theories and research. It aims to provide you with a comprehensive resource integrating educational material with practical information on how to design and implement a tailor-made approach to managing your tinnitus and related difficulties (e.g., low mood, stress, anxiety, sleep problems). Up-to-date coverage of a range of psychological techniques that have been selected on the basis of recent scientific research is presented. The techniques include cognitive therapy, attention control and imagery, relaxation training, distraction methods, and stress management. Step-by-step instructions in each of the specific techniques are provided. Detailed monitoring forms and recording sheets are included to help you keep track of your progress. This book might also be used as an adjunct to treatment offered by a professional therapist, such as a clinical psychologist, audiologist, rehabilitation counselor, or medical specialist. We hope that *Tinnitus: A Self-Management Guide for the Ringing in Your Ears* will help you acquire new skills that will change the way you think about and respond to your tinnitus, and that, in time, your tinnitus will be perceived to be less of a problem for you.

## *Acknowledgments*

We are grateful to a number of people who have contributed to our research program that has resulted in this book. We thank Maitland Bowen, Suzanne Dang, Lyndall Sullivan, Angus Forbes, Gladiss Warda, Amanda Hall, Maria Kangas, and Paul Kemp for their clinical input. We are especially grateful to Maria Kangas for her valuable and thoughtful assistance in the preparation of the final manuscript.

Particular acknowledgment must be given to all of the tinnitus patients who have participated in our research program. Their involvement and experiences have enhanced our knowledge of tinnitus.

Our gratitude is also extended to the National Health Medical Research Council for funding a multisite research project conducted at the University of New South Wales and Flinders University of South Australia.

Material presented in this book draws on the work of many researchers and clinicians in the area of clinical psychology. Many of these techniques are now accepted as part of the standard cognitive-behavior therapy approach, and we have extended and adapted these techniques to the problem of tinnitus. We wish to acknowledge explicitly the work of a number of authors in relation to specific methods or ideas, including the overall cognitive theory and therapeutic framework first advocated by Aaron T. Beck (Beck, Rush, Shaw, & Emery, 1979), upon which the whole approach is based. The work of Beck and his colleagues has been particularly influential in regard to thought-challenging techniques and the categorization of unhelpful ways of thinking (Chapters 4 and 5; see also Jakubowski & Lange, 1978). We also acknowledge the following influences in relation to thought stopping (Chapter 5; Lewinsohn, Munoz, Youngren, & Zeiss, 1978); self-instructional training (Chapter 8; Kanfer & Goldstein, 1975; Lewinsohn et al., 1978; Meichenbaum, 1975; Novaco, 1975); problem solving (Chapter 8; Nezu & Nezu, 1989); progressive muscular relaxation training (Chapter 6; Bernstein & Borkovec, 1973); increasing pleasant events (Chapter 10; Lewinsohn et al., 1978); imagery and attention control training, including the searchlight analogy and lemon-slicing example (Chapter 7; Bakal, 1982; Turk, Meichenbaum, & Genest, 1983); and relapse prevention and the identification of high-risk situations (Chapter 9; Marlatt & Gordon, 1985). Other work that has helped shape our ideas includes research on tinnitus published by Lindberg, Scott, and colleagues in Sweden (e.g., Lindberg, Scott, Melin, & Lyttkens, 1987, 1988); Hallam, Jakes, and their colleagues in the United Kingdom (e.g., Hallam, Rachman, & Hinchcliffe, 1984; Jakes, Hallam, McKenna, & Hinchcliffe, 1992; Davies, McKenna, & Hallam, 1995); and Goebel and Hiller in Germany (Goebel, Hiller, Fruhauf, & Fichter, 1992).

# 1

# *It's Time to Take Control!*

*I miss the silence. There is always the constant buzzing and humming in both of my ears. Sometimes there is also a high-pitched whistle in my left ear—that's the worst! I've had tinnitus for about five years. In the early days it wasn't too bad, but it has become worse in the last two years. Now I have no peace. I hate being in a quiet place. Night-time is the worst time—my tinnitus is all that I can hear. It is difficult to sleep and I am tired all the time. I feel so frustrated, irritable, and depressed. I find it very difficult to concentrate. I used to like working on my computer but I don't do that any more. I also enjoyed going to musical concerts and the movies. Now I can't stand all the noise. Concerts and the cinema just make my tinnitus much louder, so now I don't go. I've been to so many doctors and tried many different treatments. Nothing has given me any relief from the noise. I worry that I'll go deaf, or that the noise will drive me crazy. I feel utter despair. At times I feel so low that I just want things to end—I want to die. No one understands. I'm told that I will have to live with it, but how?*

*Tinnitus* is a term that is used to refer to the presence of sounds or noises that are perceived by a person to be located in their ears or head but that have no external cause. The noises often sound like some common environmental noise, such as a whistle, buzzing, or roaring. Tinnitus does have a physical origin; it is rarely "made up" or "imagined"—it is not a delusion. It really is there! But what causes it? The widely accepted view is that tinnitus arises from some dysfunction in the auditory or hearing mechanism. It is a relatively common problem, affecting from 6 to 17 percent of the population. Indeed, almost everyone would notice noises within their ears or head if they were placed in a totally soundproof room. Some people are not significantly troubled by tinnitus and may not even seek medical assistance. However, a significant proportion of people who experience tinnitus report considerable distress, as illustrated by the person quoted at the beginning of this chapter. It is not uncommon for people to complain of high levels of tension, anxiety, depression, irritability, and sleep difficulties. In addition to these emotional effects, tinnitus often has a significant impact on the person's social, occupational, and leisure activities. It is also a sad fact that some people who experience severe, unrelenting tinnitus are driven to suicide in a desperate attempt to rid themselves of the problem.

If you are significantly troubled by tinnitus, we advise you to consult a medical specialist. A thorough medical assessment will help to identify any conditions that could be remedied by medical or surgical intervention. For those of you whose tinnitus arises from some disorder, treatment of that disorder may reduce the tinnitus. If you have not visited a medical specialist or audiologist, we strongly urge that you make an appointment while you are reading this book.

For the vast majority of people, it is not possible to identify any precise causative disorder. This lack of identification of a specific cause is probably because the tinnitus originates in the inner ear— the place where the outside sounds are converted to neural signals that travel to the brain. This part of the ear is somewhat like the retina in the eye, where light is converted into a neural signal that is then transmitted to centers in the brain, enabling you to see the world. Failure to find a diagnosable condition does not mean that the tinnitus is "all in your head," so to speak. It just means that the exact cause cannot be linked with a known medical disorder or illness. The tinnitus has its neural origin in exactly the same place as the sounds from the environment. For some reason, this part of the inner ear, known as the *cochlea,* produces its own sound without any external source. It would be rather like the retina producing spots of light that interfere with the incoming light from the outside world. Not surprisingly, it has been very difficult to find ways to remove this problem. The area involved is microscopic and consists of intricate bundles of cells and structures, all of which are necessary for people to hear anything. Most of the traditional treatments have been shown to produce improvements in only a small proportion of people, or for very limited periods of time. Despite enormous efforts by medical researchers, there is no established, universal cure for tinnitus.

Understandably, people search relentlessly for a medical cure for their tinnitus, convinced that someone will know the answer. If you have had tinnitus for a long time, you may have gone down that path already. Along the way, you may have been told that you will need to "learn to live with the problem." If you have ever received this advice, perhaps you reacted, like many people with tinnitus, with feelings of disbelief, frustration, anger, hopelessness, and despair—all perfectly understandable. Maybe you responded to this news by renewing your search for a specialist who "has the answer." You may have tried doctor after doctor, medication after medication, and treatment after treatment, with little result. Eventually, perhaps you realized, "Well, tell me, then, how can I learn to live with this noise in my head?" Good question! This well-meaning advice to "learn to live with it" is helpful only if people are provided with assistance in achieving this goal. Unfortunately, such advice is often accompanied by another message—that "there is nothing that can be done." Although it is true that cures are rare, it is *not* true that "nothing can be done."

This book was specifically written to instruct you in a variety of techniques so that you can learn *how* to live a fulfilling life in spite of your tinnitus. The techniques that we will describe include a range of psychological or "self-control" methods that have been developed in recent years. These methods are generally referred to as *cognitive-behavioral therapy*. This term refers to the idea that by focusing on what you think (cognitive) and what you do (behavior), you can find solutions to problems—hence the name, cognitive-behavior therapy, or CBT, for short.

There is now a growing body of scientific evidence that provides support for the effectiveness of CBT in the management of a wide variety of problems. Cognitive-behavioral therapy, for example, is used to help people learn to eliminate their fears of flying, spiders, or heights, and is useful for people who are depressed or have agoraphobia. It is a major component in rehabilitation programs for chronic pain. Since the late 1980s, CBT has been used to help people with tinnitus. The aim of CBT approaches to tinnitus is to help you build on existing skills or acquire new skills to deal with your tinnitus. These skills can be applied to reduce the level of distress caused by the tinnitus and to deal with the negative consequences of the tinnitus, such as sleep difficulties, poor concentration, and interference with work, leisure, and social activities. Thus, you can reach the stage in which the tinnitus will be perceived to be less of a problem to you. In time, you may simply not notice the tinnitus because your emotional reaction to it will have been significantly reduced.

## *No. You're Not Crazy!*

From our experience, it is not uncommon for people who experience tinnitus to feel uncomfortable or unsure about the way in which psychological techniques can improve their condition. You may also be wondering what assistance these methods can provide for a medical symptom that is located in your ears! Indeed, many people react to the mere suggestion that psychological methods might be helpful as a means of managing tinnitus by insisting that their tinnitus is real and that it is not "something in their minds."

Visiting a psychologist, using psychological techniques, or even reading this book does not imply that your tinnitus is simply imagined, or that you have some "psychological problem," or that you are "crazy." People consult psychologists and use psychological techniques to assist them in dealing with a range of problems of everyday living, including dealing with stress, phobias (fears), low mood, anxiety, worry, poor sleep, stopping smoking, or weight management. People also see psychologists to learn techniques to deal with a variety of medical problems, ranging from headaches, chronic pain, high blood pressure, irritable bowel syndrome, diabetes, or a physical disability. Medical specialists assist in the medical aspects of a problem, but psychologists have a role in assisting people in adjusting to a problem and maintaining a high quality of life. Although tinnitus itself is not a psychological problem, a substantial body of research now indicates that psychological approaches to the management of this invisible symptom may help reduce tinnitus-related distress and improve the quality of a person's life.

## *Senses and Emotions: Partners in Perception*

Tinnitus is both a sensory experience *and* a sensation to which a person responds. In this regard, it is rather like pain. When you are in pain, you are aware of the physical or sensory experience of the pain. It hurts or aches, and you use words such as *piercing, burning, dull,* and *tearing* to describe the pain. People also react to pain in an emotional sense, as reflected in other words that can be used to describe pain, such as *nagging, unbearable, excruciating,* and *torturing.* Notice how the words in this last list have an emotional flavor—they are words that people use to describe other unpleasant experiences, and the words vary in the implied magnitude of the discomfort. These words neatly capture those sides of people's experiences of unpleasant sensations—the physical or sensory part and the emotional or psychological part. Tinnitus, like pain, is both a medical and a psychological phenomenon. The sounds are described as *whistling, roaring,* and *rumbling;* the reactions are described as *irritating, unbearable,* and *uncontrollable.* A person's perception of the world contains a sensory and an emotional component. As will be discussed later, it also contains a "cognitive" (thought) component—that is, people think about what they experience and it is the content of their thinking that brings about the emotional reactions.

## *Parallels between Tinnitus and Pain*

We have described tinnitus and pain in very similar terms. In fact, there are many similarities between the two experiences. Both pain and tinnitus are physical conditions that take a chronic course. A broad range of medical and alternative treatments have been applied to the management of both conditions, but most of these approaches are beneficial to only a small proportion of people. The consequences of pain and tinnitus are parallel: negative emotional states, such as depression, anxiety, and anger; sleep difficulties; and interference with interpersonal, leisure, and occupational activities. It is also quite common for people who experience either tinnitus or pain to complain about the fact that other people do not understand their problems because the symptoms are invisible. All of these difficulties have an impact on the person's psychological well-being. Many advances have been made in the management of chronic pain through the application of CBT. In a similar fashion, a great deal has been learned about psychological aspects of tinnitus, which has led to the development of interventions that can have a significant impact on the well-being and quality of life of people who are distressed by their tinnitus.

## *Common Problems Associated with Tinnitus*

It is not surprising that you might experience considerable distress if you are aware of a constant ringing, buzzing, or other type of sound in your ears or head. The precise effect that tinnitus has on people varies widely from one person to another. There are, however, a number of common problems reported by people who experience tinnitus (see Figure 1.1). Some of these problems might sound very familiar to you. Let's discuss some of them more specifically.

**FIGURE 1.1**   *Summary of Common Problems Associated with Tinnitus*

1. *Distressing Emotional Problems*
   - Tinnitus causes feelings of depression, tension, irritability, anger, annoyance, and frustration.
   - Tinnitus is worse during periods of stress.

2. *Sleep Difficulties*
   - Tinnitus causes problems in falling asleep.
   - Tinnitus makes it difficult to remain asleep.

3. *Detrimental Effects on Hearing and Communication*
   - Tinnitus makes it difficult to follow conversations or to hear what is being said against background noise.
   - Tinnitus causes problems in quiet environments.
   - Tinnitus causes problems in noisy places.

4. *Intrusiveness on Daily Activities and Lifestyle*
   - Tinnitus disrupts one's ability to concentrate on work activities and other mental tasks.
   - Tinnitus causes negative changes in relationships with spouse, partner, family members, and friends.
   - Tinnitus leads to reduced participation in work, social, and recreational activities.
   - Tinnitus leads to reduced pleasure from social, leisure, and recreational activities.

## Hearing Ability and Communication

People with tinnitus often say that the internal noise reduces their ability to listen to and understand meaningful sounds. A person may describe a difficulty in locating the source of sounds, in hearing what is being said when the background noise level is high, or in concentrating on some mental task. The effect of the tinnitus on hearing ability may be worsened if there is also some hearing loss. These problems may be a source of much frustration and distress, leading some individuals to stop participating in previously enjoyed activities and social events. Going to parties, restaurants, or the movies may become a source of annoyance rather than pleasure. This tendency toward reclusiveness and lack of opportunity to participate in enjoyable activities can lead to a lowering of mood and to feelings of helplessness and frustration. Chapter 10 will deal with some ways to overcome this problem.

## Intrusiveness of Tinnitus

Many people complain about the extent to which their tinnitus is ever-present and intrudes on their daily lives. It is not uncommon for individuals to report that they never experience any relief from the noise, making it difficult to carry out their usual daily routines. Some people comment that their tinnitus interferes with their ability to concentrate on their work; others report that work serves as a distraction. People also differ in their reactions to quiet or noisy environments. Many people avoid noisy places, not only because of the difficulty in hearing but also because it may momentarily make the tinnitus louder. This effect may be more noticeable when moving from a noisy place to a quieter place. Other people avoid quiet places because it makes the tinnitus seem to be more intrusive and reminds them that they have lost the pleasure of "silence." Thus, participation in pleasant activities such as walks in the forest or on a deserted beach may be less enjoyable because of the tinnitus. This issue will be dealt with in Chapter 10. The intrusiveness of tinnitus may also be reduced by trying some of the suggestions in Chapter 7 on attention control and imagery. In Chapter 12, we provide some more specific tips on how to deal with noisy and quiet places.

## Tinnitus-Related Fears

It is common for a person with tinnitus to fear that the tinnitus is indicative of a serious, possibly life-threatening disease; to fear that the tinnitus is the beginning of deafness; or to fear that the tinnitus may become much worse over time. If you have these fears, you will find our suggestions about dealing with "problematic thoughts" to be very helpful (see Chapters 4 and 5). We can certainly say at this point that a visit to the appropriate medical specialist is most likely to reassure you of your current physical health. Although tinnitus and hearing problems generally occur together, tinnitus often occurs with only relatively minor loss of hearing—a common part of the aging process. It is unlikely that tinnitus and hearing impairment will proceed to deafness. Although it is true that tinnitus sometimes worsens, the reverse is equally common. For most people, the tinnitus fluctuates over time, so that an apparent worsening is not necessarily a sign that the problem will continue to deteriorate.

## Anger

Some people who experience tinnitus display a great deal of anger. At times, this anger is directed at a person, company, or institution that might be responsible for causing the tinnitus. This is not uncommon when the tinnitus may have been caused by a noisy work environment. The anger may be directed at other people who do not display an adequate understanding of the tinnitus and who therefore do not provide the support that is expected. Many people with tinnitus complain that other people cannot appreciate what it is like to experience tinnitus. This may lead to tension in interpersonal relationships with partners, children, other family members, and friends. Sometimes the anger is directed at people who make loud noises or are responsible for noisy machinery, such as the truck driver who allows the air-brakes to be let off as you past by, or the neighbor who mows the lawn at inconvenient times. We have seen many people who express anger at the medical profession for failing to cure them, or against the government for not spending more money on tinnitus research. All of these reactions are understandable, but they lead the person to spend his or her energy fighting the tinnitus rather than learning ways to deal with it. A number of the approaches described in this book may be applied to manage anger. Some specific ideas for dealing with anger are provided in Chapter 12.

## *Depression*

By far the most common emotional reaction to tinnitus is a feeling of depression. By the word *depression,* we are not necessarily referring to a psychiatric disorder, but to a negative emotional mood state at the extreme end of the normal experience. People sometimes describe their feelings as sad, unhappy, miserable, or down-hearted. They may have lost their normal sense of pleasure, be less motivated, and be more pessimistic—all indications of depression. Depression often has two aspects: a sense of loss of control and a feeling of hopelessness. For most people, tinnitus does not seem to be controllable like other aspects of their lives—it is just there, relentlessly. A sense of lack of control over important aspects of life is known to be a contributor to depression. Likewise, a feeling of hopelessness is a characteristic of depression. When people feel a sense of hopelessness, they are thinking (saying to themselves) that "nothing will change," "it will get worse," "I cannot go on with this noise." The main approach to feelings of depression is outlined in Chapters 4 and 5, where we describe the central core of the CBT approach. Other suggestions are provided in Chapter 10 on "Increasing Pleasant Events."

## *Sleep Disturbance*

Some people may find that their tinnitus is not particularly bothersome during their waking hours, but complain that their tinnitus disturbs their sleep. Some individuals may experience difficulty getting to sleep, whereas others may find that they wake up frequently throughout the night and find it difficult to get back to sleep. When lying awake in bed during the night, attention is often directed toward the tinnitus because it is quiet and dark. All one can perceive is the tinnitus and how very loud it seems to be. It is easy for a person to start worrying about the tinnitus, fighting it, being annoyed by it, becoming more and more frustrated, making it all the more difficult to get to sleep. Then the person may start worrying about the consequences of a sleepless night for the following day's activities. Indeed, the inevitable fatigue and tiredness during the next day may make it more difficult to deal with the tinnitus, creating a vicious circle. Poor sleep can also be associated with a range of negative emotional states (e.g., feeling irritable, tense, uptight, depressed). On the other hand, there are people who say that sleep is their only escape from the tinnitus! If you have sleep problems, you might use a number of the approaches explained in this book. This is such a common problem that we address this more specifically in Chapter 12, but many parts of the book will be useful for dealing with this problem.

## *An Overview of Tinnitus-Related Distress*

As you can see, there are many ways in which tinnitus creates difficulties for people, quite apart from the noise itself. Once again, we see the value of distinguishing between the sensory experience of having tinnitus and the response to the tinnitus (the sound itself). In Figure 1.2 we present an overview of the way in which tinnitus leads to distress and other problems. We will use this overview to explain the process by which tinnitus may give rise to emotional distress and disruptions to daily lifestyle.

Many people who experience tinnitus say that, at times, it seems to be an overwhelming problem. You may notice that tinnitus is more difficult to deal with when you are under some sort of stress, or when you are worrying about something, or when you feel depressed or just down in the dumps. The tinnitus might also be a source of significant distress in specific situations, such as going to sleep, socializing in noisy environments, being in quiet environments, and trying to relax or concentrating on some task. At such times, the tinnitus may become more noticeable and may be more bothersome and distressing. Like many other people with tinnitus, you might think to yourself: "How can I possibly live with this?" "It's getting worse, nobody can help me!" "No one understands!" Such thoughts are very negative and distressing and can result in feeling increasingly pessimistic, out of control, and miserable. These reac-

**FIGURE 1.2** *Overview of Tinnitus-Related Distress*

---

CHRONIC TINNITUS

↑↓

**Negative Thoughts about Tinnitus**
*"How can I live with this?"*
*"The noise is getting louder."*
*"Nobody can help me."*

↓↑

**Emotional Effects**
Low mood
Depression
Irritability
Anxiety
Frustration
Tension
Anger
Helplessness

↓↑

**Disruptions to Lifestyle**
Avoidance of pleasant events/activities
Communication difficulties
Social restrictions
Disturbed sleep
Misunderstandings and relationship difficulties
Difficulties in noisy or quiet environments
Occupational difficulties

↓↑

DISTRESS

tions, in turn, might make the tinnitus seem even more unbearable, and as a consequence you may feel increasing levels of distress.

A vicious cycle can easily arise with a person feeling more and more helpless. You might experience an increasing sense of loss of control over your tinnitus, your emotions, and your thoughts. You may begin to feel more overwhelmed; you might cancel or avoid social or recreational activities, or other commitments. This may lead to the feeling that tinnitus is dictating your whole life. Furthermore, avoidance of activities may allow for more time to focus on the tinnitus. This absorption may result in even more negative thinking about the tinnitus and further emotional distress. And so the vicious cycle may continue into an ever-descending spiral! The danger of adopting this approach to tinnitus is that it may promote a sense of hopelessness, helplessness, and distress, which allows little room for dealing with the tinnitus in a more constructive manner. At some point, the spiral has to be brought under control. We assume that, if you are reading this book as someone with tinnitus, you are considering another approach. We will show you what that approach may involve after we have answered a few of the common questions about various aspects of tinnitus in the next chapter.

## *Learning How to Live with Tinnitus: Reversing the Spiral*

In this book we will provide you with instruction in a number of self-control techniques. All of these techniques can be used to begin to learn to approach the problem of tinnitus in an active and adaptive manner. It will be important for you to take an active position in response to your tinnitus and to cultivate the attitude that you will not give in to the problem—you can learn how to take control! The techniques will assist you in learning to reduce any distressing emotional effects and to reduce the impact of the tinnitus on your daily lifestyle.

This book is designed to provide you with educational and practical information on how to implement a tailor-made approach to manage your tinnitus and related difficulties. Step-by-step instruction in several specific psychological techniques will be provided. Aspects to be covered in the following chapters include the following:

**1.** *Information about the Nature of Tinnitus*
In the next chapter some factual information about tinnitus will be presented. We will describe what it is, some common terms that people use to describe the sounds, what causes it, and some of the available medical and audiological treatments.

**2.** *How to Assess the Impact of Your Tinnitus*
In Chapter 3 we will outline some practical exercises to help you determine the specific ways in which tinnitus has affected you and your life. The first step in designing your own individual program will be understanding how tinnitus has had an impact on your emotions, behavior, and activities. In order for you to set out to change the way in which you respond to your tinnitus, you need to identify what tinnitus has done to your life, the way in which it affects you, and the way in which you currently react to your tinnitus.

**3.** *Cognitive Therapy*
Cognitive therapy is a specific set of techniques aimed to help you to change your ways of thinking. It has emerged as the main psychological technique that may be helpful for people with tinnitus. This therapy has evolved out of the cognitive theory of emotions that asserts that the influence of a situation or event experienced by a person is through the way a person perceives (or thinks about) the event, not the event itself. Cognitive therapy was originally developed as a treatment of emotional states, such as depression and anxiety. More recently, it has been successfully applied to chronic pain and other medical problems, such as tinnitus. According to the cognitive theory, the source of distress for a person with tinnitus is the way in which the person *perceives* the tinnitus. A person who engages in constructive thoughts in response to his or her tinnitus—such as "the noise won't harm me," "it is not pleasant but I can deal with it," or "I'd

rather the noise would go away but I can control it"—is less likely to experience high levels of distress. On the other hand, a person who thinks negative thoughts—such as "I can't live with this," "something must be terribly wrong," or "the noise will drive me crazy"—will be more likely to experience negative emotional states (e.g., anxiety, depression, hopelessness). You can learn to identify the content of your thoughts (beliefs, attitudes, perceptions) in response to your tinnitus and to develop your own ways of constructively dealing with these thoughts. Specific instruction in this process is provided in Chapter 5.

There are also approaches that are designed to help you more directly with the sensory experience of tinnitus. These approaches involve attention control and imagery training (described in Chapter 7). Through these methods, you can learn other forms of cognitive therapy that aim to alter attentional processes through imagery or redirection of attention. These approaches are useful in helping you to learn ways to shift the focus of your attention away from your tinnitus, which may lead to a greater sense of control.

**4.** *Relaxation Techniques*
Many people with tinnitus report that there is a relationship between their tinnitus and stress. Some complain that their tinnitus makes them feel nervous and tense. Others comment that their tinnitus becomes worse during periods of physical or emotional stress, or when they are fatigued. Relaxation techniques may be helpful on these occasions and they are also useful in managing sleep problems. A number of relaxation procedures are described in Chapter 6.

## Conclusion

The aim of this book is to provide a comprehensive self-help guide for people with tinnitus. The techniques described in this book are generally referred to as cognitive-behavioral therapy. There is now a growing body of evidence that supports the effectiveness of these techniques. The aim of these approaches to tinnitus is to reduce the negative impact of tinnitus on your life and to lead to a state in which the tinnitus will be perceived to be less of a problem.

It is important to remember that all of the techniques described in this book require extensive practice in order for you to develop skill and expertise in applying the approaches. Learning any new skill (e.g., learning to play a musical instrument, play a sport, use a computer, etc.) involves some period of conscious effort. You will need to approach the skills described in this book in much the same way. The more frequently you practice the skills, the greater the rewards will be. To assist you with this practice, we have provided detailed monitoring forms for you to record your practice and to help you monitor your progress. We suggest that you photocopy the monitoring forms we have provided so that you can keep an ongoing record of your practice sessions with each particular skill you will be learning.

With regular practice and increased skill, people generally report that they experience significant reductions in tinnitus-related distress. By acquiring effective coping skills, you can change your emotional reaction to tinnitus. Eventually, these skills should become so automatic that you are barely aware that you are using the suggestions in this book, and you may often be unaware of your tinnitus. When you find yourself advising someone else with tinnitus that they should try out these ideas, you will know that you have made very significant progress in dealing with your own tinnitus.

# 2

# *Some Facts about Tinnitus*

*About 12 months ago I became aware of noises in my left ear. There is a mixture of sounds. I hear a hissing sound like steam escaping, mixed in with a shuddering thud, a bit like the sound of water rushing or rattling through pipes. At first the noises would come and go. There just didn't seem to be any explanation for why the sound would change. I felt such relief when I couldn't hear it. I'd go for days, even weeks, without any noise. I even thought that I might have been imagining it. Then suddenly I'd wake up one day and the noise would be back. About eight months ago it became more constant. This really frightened me. I wondered what the hell it meant! My first thought was that the noise must be a sign that I have something physically wrong with me—something serious. All I could think was: What is this? What does it mean? Will it ever go away?*

## *What Is Tinnitus?*

The word *tinnitus* is derived from the Latin word *tinnire* and means "to tinkle or ring like a bell." Tinnitus is a subjective experience of hearing a sound, usually located in the ear(s) and/or head, when no such external physical sound is present. People use a wide variety of commonly encountered sounds to describe their tinnitus. Some common subjective descriptors include *buzzing, hissing, ocean*

**17**

*waves, clicking, pulsing, ringing, pounding, chirping, clanging, insects, musical tones, rushing, sizzling, roaring, whistling, whining,* and *humming.* The person may be aware of only one sound or may be able to hear several different types of sounds, even in one ear. The sound, which may be heard in one ear only or in both ears, may also appear to come from different locations inside the head, or it may appear to come from outside the head. Tinnitus may be relatively constant in loudness or it may vary over time, becoming louder or softer at different times throughout the day. Some people may perceive the loudness of their tinnitus to alter partly as a function of changes in the loudness of background noise. The overall loudness may appear to increase or decrease over longer time frames, across many months or years.

## How Common Is Tinnitus?

Relatively continuous tinnitus is estimated to be experienced by about 6 to 17 percent of people. About 1 to 2 percent of the population experience severe distress associated with the problem. People of all ages may experience tinnitus, including children. The incidence of tinnitus up to the age of 30 to 40 years is relatively low, and increases above the age of 40. In most people, tinnitus is associated with other hearing problems, and it is common for people with tinnitus to have at least a mild hearing loss.

## What Causes Tinnitus?

Many of the broad causes of tinnitus are produced by the environment. Hazardous noise exposure arising from a wide variety of recreational and occupational sources is one of the most common causes of tinnitus. Rock music concerts, listening to stereos, and shooting are potential sources of recreational noise exposure. Occupational noise exposure may include working with machinery, such as jackhammers or electric drills; using headphones; and even playing musical instruments in an orchestra or band. Military service is another potential source of noise exposure. Damage to the auditory system may result from either chronic noise exposure over a long period or from acute trauma that can occur when a person experiences a single brief exposure to hazardous noise (e.g., arising from faulty equipment or an explosion).

A second common and well-established cause of tinnitus is the high-frequency hearing loss associated with advancing age, which is known as *presbycusis*. Tinnitus can also be the result of numerous problems in the auditory system or hearing mechanism. For example, Meniére's disease is characterized by episodic vertigo, hearing loss, tinnitus, and a feeling of fullness or pressure in the ear.

Many medications produce tinnitus as an undesirable side effect. Quinine and other anti-malarial medications, as well as a high dosage of aspirin, may produce temporary tinnitus and hearing loss. Other substances that may be associated with tinnitus include some diuretics, antibiotics, antidepressants, salt, nicotine, alcohol, caffeine, tonic water, and heavy metals (e.g., lead or mercury poisoning).

Tinnitus may also be associated with a number of medical conditions, such as various vascular and arterial problems, dental problems, jaw muscle malfunction, cardiovascular disease, arteriosclerosis, thyroid disorders, diabetes, tumors, and neuromas, among others. Also, head injuries or traumatic blows to the head as the result of automobile accident injuries, whiplash, or concussion may produce transient or chronic tinnitus.

## What Treatments Are Available for Tinnitus?

Several forms of treatment are currently available, some of which may provide relief to some people. Every person with tinnitus should be examined by an ear, nose, and throat specialist (an otologist or otolaryngologist) in order to identify whether any conditions are present that could be remedied by medication or surgical intervention. This evaluation should also be accompanied by a comprehensive hearing assessment, normally conducted by an audiologist. This evaluation is needed to determine the person's hearing capability and to identify whether the tinnitus might be relieved through the use of some audiological or hearing-aid device. Specific tinnitus assessment may include testing for the pitch and loudness of the tinnitus through tasks that involve matching the internal sounds with external ones, generally delivered through headphones.

## Medical Treatments

For those people whose tinnitus arises from some identifiable causative or related disorder (e.g., Meniére's disease, hypertension, diabetes, hypothyroidism) treatment of the medical disorder may reduce the impact of the tinnitus. For the majority of people, however, it is not feasible to identify any precise causative disorder, although it can be assumed that, in most cases, there is damage to the so-called hair cells in the cochlea, located in the inner ear. Numerous types of medications have been investigated as possible treatments for tinnitus. These medications include various anesthetics, anticonvulsants, and vasodilators. Other medical treatments for tinnitus include surgery, generally performed in order to correct some underlying process or disease that may ultimately influence the tinnitus. Electrical suppression and cochlear implantation have also been used, somewhat rarely, as methods to relieve tinnitus. Although some medications and surgical interventions have been found to be useful for some people, at this point there is no specific medication or medical intervention that can be universally recommended as a treatment for tinnitus. If you wish to know more about the treatments that have been used, you might benefit from reading some of the material that is recommended in the final section of this book.

## Audiological Treatments

Audiological approaches to the management of tinnitus include the use of masking devices, hearing aids, and combinations of both devices (known as a *tinnitus instrument*). Tinnitus maskers are small devices that are worn like a hearing aid and deliver a continuous band of noise into the ear. The masking may cover or reduce the person's perception of the tinnitus sound. Being an external sound, it may be more acceptable to the person and may be more easily ignored. Although not a cure for tinnitus, masking may provide some relief. Some people discover natural sources of masking that provide relief from their tinnitus, such as the sound of electric fans or music. Other people say that it is useful to set an FM radio between stations because this setting produces static that makes the tinnitus less audible. This simple procedure might provide sufficient masking when needed (e.g., prior to sleep or during periods of concentration), reducing the need for more intensive approaches.

The fitting of a hearing aid in people who have a marked hearing loss can prove to have beneficial effects for some people with tinnitus. A hearing aid may amplify background noise to the extent that the tinnitus is effectively masked by natural environmental sound. Many people with tinnitus and hearing loss complain of the effect of the tinnitus on their comprehension in conversations. The restoration of hearing by the aid may result in improvements in the ability to understand and engage in conversations.

A thorough discussion of the various medical, surgical, and audiological treatments available for tinnitus is beyond the scope of this book. We wish to emphasize that it is critical for each person with tinnitus to seek consultation with a medical specialist and audiologist to discuss the options that are available.

## *Conclusion*

In this chapter we presented some basic, factual information about tinnitus. When you first became aware of your tinnitus, you may have been puzzled about the meaning and causes of these sounds. You might find some of the reading material listed at the end of this book to be useful. If we have not covered some aspect of tinnitus that is causing you some concern, we suggest that you take the time to discuss this aspect of the problem with your medical specialist.

In order to begin the process of acquiring effective self-control skills to manage your tinnitus, you first need to understand the specific ways in which it affects you personally. The next chapter will help you to assess the impact of your tinnitus on your emotions, thoughts, and activities. Subsequent chapters will provide you with step-by-step instructions in some specific techniques to learn to manage your tinnitus and other related difficulties.

# 3

## *Assessing Your Tinnitus*

### *How Does It Affect You?*

*I have had tinnitus for about 20 years. I hear a constant ringing sound in both my ears. I must admit that I cannot bear being in quiet places where there is not much sound. I find this very difficult. I always have to have some noise around me. When I am at home I will have the TV on in the background. At work, my office is very quiet, so I always have the radio on or play a CD on my computer. Having external sound around me constantly seems to help block out the noises in my head. Even when I go to sleep I will listen to my Walkman radio. Over the years I have met other people who have tinnitus. Some people cannot seem to understand why I need to have other noise in the background. They seem to think that it is enough just having to put up with a constant noise in their ears. Some people seem to go to great lengths to avoid noise. I find this surprising!*

In Chapter 1 we looked at some of the common problems that are often associated with tinnitus (e.g., emotional distress, sleep difficulties, reduced participation in leisure and social activities, and concentration problems). However, research reveals that people with tinnitus vary considerably in the nature and extent of the problems they experience. Assessing the precise ways in which tinnitus affects you as an individual is an important first step in designing and implementing your own tailor-made self-management program.

In this chapter we provide a number of self-assessment exercises for you to complete in order to identify the impact of your tinnitus on your emotions, behavior, thoughts, and well-being. These exercises will require some work on your part and will involve completing some questionnaires about the specific ways that tinnitus affects you and your life. This information-collecting is crucial to any successful program. If you consulted a psychologist, this type of assessment would be conducted at the outset. We believe that, with the guidance provided here, many readers will be able to perform this assessment for themselves and begin the process of self-management of the problem. Through the process of self-monitoring, you will gain a better understanding of the way in which the specific techniques that are covered in this book may apply to you personally. The information that you collect from completing the self-assessment exercises will help you to identify exactly what areas you need to tackle and where to begin to design your own individually tailored self-management program.

## *Self-Assessment Exercise 1: How Does Your Tinnitus Affect You?*

Figure 3.1 presents a copy of the Tinnitus Reaction Questionnaire, which is designed to assess the specific difficulties that you might experience as a result of having tinnitus. The items cover a range of effects that tinnitus may have on your emotions, lifestyle, and general well-being. This questionnaire has been used extensively in our research on tinnitus.

### What Can You Learn from the Tinnitus Reaction Questionnaire?

If you wish to obtain a total score on the Tinnitus Reaction Questionnaire, you simply add up all the numbers that you circled. First

**FIGURE 3.1**  *Self-Assessment Exercise 1:*
*Tinnitus Reaction Questionnaire*

---

This questionnaire is designed to find out what sort of effects tinnitus has on your emotions, lifestyle, and general well-being. Some of the effects listed here may well apply to you; others may not. Please be sure that you answer each question by circling the number that best reflects how your tinnitus has affected you over the *past week*.

0 = Not at all
1 = A little of the time
2 = Some of the time
3 = A good deal of the time
4 = Almost all the time

| | | | | | | |
|---|---|---|---|---|---|---|
| 1. | My tinnitus has made me unhappy. | 0 | 1 | 2 | 3 | 4 |
| 2. | My tinnitus has made me feel tense. | 0 | 1 | 2 | 3 | 4 |
| 3. | My tinnitus has made me feel irritable. | 0 | 1 | 2 | 3 | 4 |
| 4. | My tinnitus has made me feel angry. | 0 | 1 | 2 | 3 | 4 |
| 5. | My tinnitus has led me to cry. | 0 | 1 | 2 | 3 | 4 |
| 6. | My tinnitus has led me to avoid quiet situations. | 0 | 1 | 2 | 3 | 4 |
| 7. | My tinnitus has made me feel less interested in going out. | 0 | 1 | 2 | 3 | 4 |
| 8. | My tinnitus has made me feel depressed. | 0 | 1 | 2 | 3 | 4 |
| 9. | My tinnitus has made me feel annoyed. | 0 | 1 | 2 | 3 | 4 |
| 10. | My tinnitus has made me feel confused. | 0 | 1 | 2 | 3 | 4 |
| 11. | My tinnitus has "driven me crazy." | 0 | 1 | 2 | 3 | 4 |
| 12. | My tinnitus has interfered with my enjoyment of life. | 0 | 1 | 2 | 3 | 4 |
| 13. | My tinnitus has made it hard for me to concentrate. | 0 | 1 | 2 | 3 | 4 |
| 14. | My tinnitus has made it hard for me to relax. | 0 | 1 | 2 | 3 | 4 |
| 15. | My tinnitus has made me feel distressed. | 0 | 1 | 2 | 3 | 4 |
| 16. | My tinnitus has made me feel helpless. | 0 | 1 | 2 | 3 | 4 |
| 17. | My tinnitus has made me feel frustrated with things. | 0 | 1 | 2 | 3 | 4 |
| 18. | My tinnitus has interfered with my ability to work. | 0 | 1 | 2 | 3 | 4 |
| 19. | My tinnitus has led me to despair. | 0 | 1 | 2 | 3 | 4 |
| 20. | My tinnitus has led me to avoid noisy situations. | 0 | 1 | 2 | 3 | 4 |
| 21. | My tinnitus has led me to avoid social situations. | 0 | 1 | 2 | 3 | 4 |
| 22. | My tinnitus has made me feel hopeless about the future. | 0 | 1 | 2 | 3 | 4 |
| 23. | My tinnitus has interfered with my sleep. | 0 | 1 | 2 | 3 | 4 |
| 24. | My tinnitus has led me to think about suicide. | 0 | 1 | 2 | 3 | 4 |
| 25. | My tinnitus has made me feel panicky. | 0 | 1 | 2 | 3 | 4 |
| 26. | My tinnitus has made me feel tormented. | 0 | 1 | 2 | 3 | 4 |

---

make sure that you have circled one number (and only one number) for each item. Now add up the numbers. The possible scores range from 0 to 104. If your score is between 0 and 16, this rating would suggest that you are managing very well with your tinnitus. If your score is above 16, you are likely to gain a great deal from reading this book. However, we also recommend that you consult with a medical and/or health professional (e.g., medical specialist or clinical psychologist), particularly if you feel that you are not coping with your tinnitus. Perhaps you could take this book with you to the professional whom you visit. The ideas in this book may be incorporated within a professionally structured treatment program.

Now go back and examine the individual items from the questionnaire. You will need to be a little cautious about interpreting the individual items, since we know that these will sometimes shift from one administration of this test to another while the total score remains the same. You could always repeat this test tomorrow and see how stable your responses are to the individual items.

Items 1 to 5, 8 to 11, 14 to 17, 19, 22, and 24 to 26 can be added to obtain a score that reflects the emotional reactions to tinnitus. These items are composed of different emotions, including depression, anxiety, and anger. If you endorse a large number of these items, you may find that the techniques described in Chapters 4 and 5 are especially useful to reduce symptoms of emotional distress. These approaches can be combined with relaxation techniques to address symptoms of stress, anxiety, and tension (see Chapter 6).

Items 6, 7, 12, 13, 18, 20, and 21 are concerned with "interference"—that is, the extent to which tinnitus interferes with your work, social situations, and recreational activities. If you endorse many of the items in this part of the questionnaire, we suggest that you pay particular attention to Chapter 10, which describes ways to increase your participation in pleasant events.

Item 23 is concerned with sleep disturbance. If you obtained a score of either 3 or 4 on this single item, you may wish to examine your sleep more closely on the specially constructed form shown later in this chapter. Depending on the outcome, you might find the material on cognitive therapy, attention control, and relaxation especially useful for dealing with sleep problems (see Chapters 4 to 7). Additional tips on improving your sleep are in Chapter 12.

Items 22 and 24 are concerned with feelings of hopelessness and suicidal thoughts. If you obtained a score of 3 or 4 on either of these items, we suggest that you consider seeking more formal assistance with your tinnitus problem, especially if you have obtained a high score on the overall test. It might also be useful at this point to read the section on suicide in Chapter 12.

## *Self-Assessment Exercise 2: How Does Your Tinnitus Affect Your Mood?*

Another method of collecting valuable information about the precise ways that your tinnitus affects your mood, well-being, and daily

**FIGURE 3.2**   *Self-Assessment Exercise 2: Tinnitus Daily Diary*

Day: _____   Date: _____

1. Today, I noticed my tinnitus: (Circle one)

   Not at all     A little of      Some           A good deal      Almost all
                  the time        of the time     of the time      the time

2. Today, the loudest my tinnitus got was: (Circle one)

   No tinnitus    Very faint      Moderately loud    Very loud     Extremely loud

3. Was there any situation or time when your tinnitus was very noticeable? If so, please give details:

   _____

   _____

4. Today, my tinnitus bothered or annoyed me: (Circle one)

   Not at all     A little     Moderately     Very much     Extremely

5. Today, my tinnitus made me feel tense or uptight: (Circle one)

   Not at all     A little     Moderately     Very much     Extremely

6. Today, my tinnitus made me feel irritable or angry: (Circle one)

   Not at all     A little     Moderately     Very much     Extremely routine is to begin to keep a daily diary. Use the Tinnitus Daily Diary described in Figure 3.2 to help you to complete Self-Assessment Exercise 2. We recommend that you complete the diary over a couple of weeks. Figure 3.3 describes how you can use the information that you collect by keeping a Tinnitus Daily Diary.

**FIGURE 3.3**  *How to Use the Information Obtained in Your Tinnitus Daily Diary*

When examining the information that you have recorded in your diary there are a number of things that you might look for:

1. In what specific ways does your tinnitus affect your mood?

   _____

   _____

   _____

   _____

2. Does it make you feel tense or uptight?

   If yes, you may benefit from reading the material on relaxation techniques that are described in Chapter 6.

3. Does it produce other symptoms of emotional distress (e.g., feeling annoyed, irritable, angry)?

   If yes, relaxation techniques could be used in combination with the cognitive methods described in Chapters 4 and 5, and various other strategies described in this book.

4. Are there any regular patterns or relationships between events that occur during the day and changes in your mood or your tinnitus? (Some examples might include the following: tinnitus is worse when you are tired; you feel down when you have too much to do; when you are working, your tinnitus is louder.) Try to identify the pattern and describe this in the space below:

   _____

   _____

**FIGURE 3.3**  *Continued*

_____

_____

_____

**5.** Are there any specific situations when your tinnitus is more noticeable? (Some examples might include that you find it more noticeable whenever you are in a noisy place, when you are trying to concentrate on some task at work, or when you are dealing with some stressful situation.)

If yes, list these in the space provided below:

_____

_____

_____

_____

We suggest some strategies that might be useful for dealing with problem situations in Chapter 9 (dealing with high-risk situations). A combination of several of the techniques described in Chapters 4 through to 8 might assist you in preparing effective plans to help deal with these specific situations.

**6.** Are there any specific times of the day when your tinnitus is more noticeable?

If yes, try to identify exactly what is happening at these times and write these details in the space provided below. (For example, you might notice that your tinnitus is worse in the morning when you are trying to juggle a number of things, such as preparing breakfast, making lunch for your children, feeding the dog, getting ready for work, dealing with peak-hour traffic, getting the children off to school, and so on). Alternatively, it might be worse during quiet times of the day, (such as when you get into bed and try to get to sleep, or when relaxing).

_____

_____

_____

_____

*Continued*

**FIGURE 3.3**   *Continued*

_____

_____

_____

If you do identify a specific time of the day when your tinnitus is worse, a combination of the self-control techniques described in Chapters 4 through to 9 should
prove to be useful. We offer some suggestions for dealing with quiet environments and sleep difficulties in Chapter 12.

7. Can you see any particular pattern—for example, is your tinnitus worse on certain days of the week?

   If yes, think about what happens on those days. Are there particular events that
   occur on those days that might make things worse? (For example, you might find
   that your tinnitus is worse on Mondays, as your working week begins with a
   stressful meeting with your supervisor to discuss goals for the week; you might
   notice that it is worse on Wednesdays when you always have back-to-back
   appointments; or you might notice that it is worse on certain days when you have
   to do certain tasks, or interact with certain people.) Now, in the space below, try
   to describe any specific events that occur on those days when your tinnitus is
   worse.

   _____

   _____

   _____

   _____

   _____

8. Is your tinnitus worse during the week, as compared to the weekend?

   If yes, why might this be so? Try to identify some reasons, and write these in the
   space below. (For example, is it because on the weekends, you feel more
   relaxed, you can enjoy more pleasurable activities, and you don't experience as
   much pressure?)

   _____

   _____

**FIGURE 3.3** *Continued*

_____

_____

_____

**9.** Is your tinnitus better during the week, as compared to the weekend?

If yes, why might this be so? Try to identify some reasons, and write these in the space below. (For example, is it because you are too busy during the week to notice your tinnitus, you have too many distractions during the week, or you really don't do very much on the weekend so there is more time to focus on your tinnitus?)

_____

_____

_____

_____

_____

**10.** As well as looking for factors that might make your tinnitus worse, you can use your diary to try to identify what factors might make it better. (Some examples might include the following: when you watched the football game you weren't bothered by your tinnitus; when you were enjoying the music at the concert you didn't notice your tinnitus; when you are feeling good about life in general, the tinnitus isn't a problem.)

Look closely at those days when you didn't notice your tinnitus, when it wasn't especially loud, or when it didn't trouble you. Think back over the day. What were you doing? How were you feeling? Why do you think it was such a good day? What specific things made your tinnitus better?

_____

_____

_____

_____

## *Self-Assessment Exercise 3: How Does Your Tinnitus Affect Your Sleep?*

One of the most common difficulties reported by people with tinnitus is sleep disturbance. Some people report difficulty getting to sleep; others report that they fall asleep without much trouble but they experience frequent awakenings through the night; and still others say that sleep is their only escape from the constant noise! In order to assess whether your tinnitus affects your sleep, complete the sleep diary provided in Figure 3.4. We suggest that you keep

**FIGURE 3.4  *Self-Assessment Exercise 3: Sleep Daily Diary Recording Sheet***

Day: _____     Date:_____

1.  How difficult was it for you to get to sleep last night? (Circle one)

    | Not at all difficult | A little difficult | Fairly difficult | Quite difficult | Very difficult |

2.  If you had any difficulty getting to sleep last night, was this: (Circle one)

    Mainly because of tinnitus     Partly due to tinnitus     Some other reason

3.  How restless was your sleep? (Circle one)

    | Not at all restless | A little restless | Fairly restless | Quite restless | Very restless |

4.  If your sleep was restless, was this: (Circle one)

    Mainly because of tinnitus     Partly due to tinnitus     Some other reason

5.  If your sleep was interrupted during the night because of your tinnitus, what thoughts did you notice running through your mind at these times? Write those thoughts here.

    _____

    _____

    _____

your diary next to your bed and complete it as soon as you get out of bed in the morning. Try to complete the diary over a couple of consecutive weeks. Your diary should provide you with information to answer the questions presented in Figure 3.5. The relaxation training and attentional control methods described in Chapters 6 and 7 may be especially useful if you experience sleep problems. The cognitive methods might also prove to be very useful (see Chapters 4 and 5). In Chapter 12 we offer some more specific tips for dealing with poor sleep.

**FIGURE 3.5** *How Does Tinnitus Affect Your Sleep?*

Use the information that you have collected in your sleep diary to answer the following questions:

1. Does your tinnitus make it difficult for you to get to sleep?

   _____

2. How long does it normally take you to fall asleep (i.e., on a "good" night)?

   _____

3. Is your sleep interrupted by tinnitus in the middle of the night? If yes, how often?

   _____

4. How do you feel when you wake with loud tinnitus?

   _____

5. What thoughts are going through your mind when you awaken and notice your tinnitus?

   _____

6. Do you recall having sleep difficulties before you developed tinnitus?

   _____

# Self-Assessment Exercise 4: What Kinds of Thoughts Do You Have When You Notice Your Tinnitus?

We have already mentioned the important connection between the way people think in response to their tinnitus and their emotional state. A very important strategy to manage tinnitus is to learn to think constructive thoughts in response to your tinnitus and to learn to control negative automatic thoughts (see Chapters 4 and 5). However, the first step in learning to control the way you think is to become aware of the kinds of thoughts that you engage in when you notice your tinnitus. Figure 3.6 presents a copy of a questionnaire called the Tinnitus Cognitions Questionnaire. Read the instructions and complete the questionnaire to begin to identify some of the thoughts that you might think in response to your tinnitus.

**Figure 3.6** *Self-Assessment Exercise 4: Tinnitus Cognitions Questionnaire*

---

In this questionnaire we would like to know what kinds of thoughts come into your head when you notice your tinnitus. Some of the thoughts you have might be rather negative and others might be more positive. You might not necessarily think all the thoughts listed below, but you may recognize some that apply to you. Please indicate how often you have been aware of thinking a particular thought on occasions when you have noticed the tinnitus.

    0 = Never
    1 = Rarely
    2 = Occasionally
    3 = Frequently
    4 = Very Frequently

**The first ones are the more *negative* thoughts that you might have.**

1. I think, "If only the noise would go away."                          0  1  2  3  4
2. I think, "Why me? Why do I have to suffer this horrible noise?"       0  1  2  3  4
3. I think, "What did I do to deserve this?"                            0  1  2  3  4
4. I think, "The noise makes my life unbearable."                       0  1  2  3  4
5. I think, "Nobody understands how bad the noise is."                  0  1  2  3  4
6. I think, "If only I could get some peace and quiet."                 0  1  2  3  4
7. I think, "I can't enjoy what I'm doing because of the noise."        0  1  2  3  4

## FIGURE 3.6  *Continued*

| | |
|---|---|
| **8.** I think, "How can I go on putting up with this noise?" | 0  1  2  3  4 |
| **9.** I think, "The noise will drive me crazy." | 0  1  2  3  4 |
| **10.** I think, "Why can't anyone help me?" | 0  1  2  3  4 |
| **11.** I think, "My tinnitus is never going to get better." | 0  1  2  3  4 |
| **12.** I think, "The noise will overwhelm me." | 0  1  2  3  4 |
| **13.** I think, "With this noise, life is not worth living." | 0  1  2  3  4 |

**Now, here are the more *positive* thoughts that you might have:**

| | |
|---|---|
| **14.** I think, "No matter how unpleasant the noise gets, I can cope." | 0  1  2  3  4 |
| **15.** I think, "The noise might be unpleasant, but it won't drive me crazy." | 0  1  2  3  4 |
| **16.** I think, "I'll be able to enjoy things more if I keep my attention off the noise." | 0  1  2  3  4 |
| **17.** I think, "I'm not the only person with tinnitus." | 0  1  2  3  4 |
| **18.** I think, "There are things in life worse than tinnitus." | 0  1  2  3  4 |
| **19.** I think, "The noise will eventually get less annoying if I try to distract myself from it." | 0  1  2  3  4 |
| **20.** I think, "I have coped with the noise before, so I can cope again this time." | 0  1  2  3  4 |
| **21.** I say to myself, "It will help if I try to think of something pleasant." | 0  1  2  3  4 |
| **22.** I tell myself, "I can learn to live with it." | 0  1  2  3  4 |
| **23.** I think, "The noise might be there, but I can still enjoy things." | 0  1  2  3  4 |
| **24.** I tell myself, "Think of something else other than the noise." | 0  1  2  3  4 |
| **25.** I tell myself, "I won't think about the noise." | 0  1  2  3  4 |
| **26.** I think, "The noise is a nuisance, but I just won't let it bother me." | 0  1  2  3  4 |

## How Can You Use the Tinnitus Cognitions Questionnaire?

If you wish, you can calculate two separate scores for the Tinnitus Cognitions Questionnaire—one for negative thoughts and one for positive thoughts. First, make sure that you have circled one number (and only one number) for each of the 26 items. For the negative thoughts (questions 1 to 13), you simply add up all the numbers that you circled alongside the negative thoughts. The possible scores range from 0 to 52. Now for the positive thoughts (questions

14 to 26), you simply add up all the numbers that you circled along-side the positive thoughts. A score of approximately 23 is average. The "ideal" pattern of response would be a low score on the negative thoughts section and a high score on the positive thoughts section.

There are several possible categories of response to the Tinnitus Cognitions Questionnaire. You may find that you have a high score on the negative thoughts section and a low score on the positive thoughts section. This pattern of response would indicate that you engage in quite a lot of thinking about your tinnitus that is negative and unconstructive. Another pattern of responses involves a similar amount of negative and positive thinking about the tinnitus (high score on both sections). This pattern of response would suggest that you either (1) attempt to reduce the negative thoughts by engaging in positive countering thoughts or (2) find yourself thinking more negatively or more positively on different occasions. In either case, you may be part of the way along the path that we are advocating in this book. If your responses reveal that you tend to think a large number of negative thoughts, we recommend that you read the material in the next two chapters. These chapters show how you can manage negative thoughts and change the way that you think in response to your tinnitus.

## Self-Assessment Exercise 5: To What Extent Has Tinnitus Interfered with Your Daily Activities?

A considerable number of people often complain about the extent to which tinnitus interferes with their daily activities (e.g., leisure, social, occupational) or leads them to avoid certain activities (e.g., noisy places, quiet places). Thus, one other aspect that you need to consider is whether certain activities are being affected by your tinnitus. Figure 3.7 presents some questions that you might ask yourself concerning the impact of your tinnitus on your activity level. In Chapter 10 we describe some methods to increase your participation in pleasant activities so as to reduce the impact of tinnitus on

**FIGURE 3.7**   *Self-Assessment Exercise 5: Assessing the Impact of Tinnitus on Your Activity Level*

Consider each of the following questions. List any of your daily activities that might have been disrupted by your tinnitus. For each affected activity, indicate how frequently this problem occurs and try to identify the reasons why this happens.

1. To what extent have any of your leisure or work activities been affected by your tinnitus?

    Examples:

    I can't concentrate on my computer for lengthy periods of time.

    I avoid going to orchestral concerts.

    I have to have frequent breaks at work.

    I don't play my musical instrument anymore.

2. Do you ever decide not to go somewhere because of your tinnitus?

    Examples:

    I no longer go to the movies or to concerts.

    If my tinnitus is bad I will cancel any social participation.

    When my tinnitus is very loud I may stay home from work.

*Continued*

**FIGURE 3.7** *Continued*

_____

_____

_____

3. Do you ever decide not to do something because of your tinnitus?
   Examples:

   When my tinnitus is annoying I avoid doing anything.
   _____
   If my tinnitus is bad I will avoid being with my friends because they don't understand.
   _____
   I make a conscious effort to avoid any noisy environment—loud music, heavy
   traffic, loud machinery.
   _____

   _____

   _____

   _____

   _____

   _____

4. Does the tinnitus cause you to avoid noisy situations?
   Examples:

   I avoid noisy clubs and bars.
   _____
   I avoid going on airplanes or trains.
   _____
   No, I seek out places with noise in the background to mask my tinnitus.
   _____

   _____

   _____

   _____

   _____

**FIGURE 3.7** *Continued*

5. Does the tinnitus cause you to avoid quiet places?
   Examples:

   I always have to have some noise in the background; the radio or an electric fan
   helps.

   At night-time I listen to my portable stereo.

your lifestyle. In Chapter 12 we offer some specific tips on dealing with noisy and quiet environments.

## *Conclusion*

You have now taken the first step in your self-management program. The information that you have collected by completing the exercises in this chapter should give you a clearer picture of the way in which the tinnitus has affected you, with respect to mood, negative thoughts, sleep disturbance, activities, and so forth. In the next chapter, we take this level of analysis a step further. In particular, we examine the ways in which your thinking affects the way in which you experience the tinnitus.

# 4

# *The Connection between Thoughts and Emotions*

*A snapshot of thoughts:*

*Another hectic day! I just want to put my feet up and relax. First I'll check the mailbox. Probably only bills. This one looks like a card. I wonder who sent it? It's from John! What a pleasant surprise! I didn't expect him to remember my birthday....It's so good to be home...Gosh! What was that noise? Sounds like someone in the house—what if it's a burglar!*

## *The Cognitive Theory of Emotions*

The suggestions in this book are based on a particular theory called the *cognitive theory.* This theory attempts to account for the way people feel at any given moment—for example, feelings of happiness, depression, anger, guilt, or fear. Why do people experience these feelings? The cognitive theory proposes that these feelings arise from the specific content of the thoughts that run through people's minds from moment to moment. Everyone has these thoughts—there is nothing unusual about them. Indeed, it would be unusual if people didn't think about anything as they go about their daily activities. The person who is describing his or her thoughts in the opening of this chapter provides a typical example.

The cognitive theory suggests that the content of these thoughts leads to the experience of specific emotions. In the chapter-opening example, the person mentions hearing a noise in the house and thinks, "What if it's a burglar!" What emotion do you think this person experiences at that point? If you think "fear," you are probably correct. When the person found the unexpected birthday card in the mailbox, he or she thought, "What a pleasant surprise!" The emotion? Probably happiness. We say "probably" because it is not always the case that the same event will have the same effect on another person. The different thought content probably determines the difference between people. Someone else, upon receiving the birthday card, might think, "John just sent it to remind me that I forgot to send him a card for his birthday—he is just getting back at me." That person might actually feel angry that he or she received the card. Anyone who has seen the popular television series, *Ally McBeal,* will likely have noticed that the main character often has her thoughts dubbed into the script—viewers hear them, but the other characters cannot eavesdrop! Well, that idea is exactly the point that we are trying to make here.

Throughout the day a person experiences a range of events. For example, the clock radio goes on, you get out of bed, you make breakfast, the telephone rings, you miss the train, your business meeting is successful, you share a joke with a friend, you misplace your keys, and so on. During a day a person also experiences changes in the way they feel, such as feeling irritable, happy, annoyed, sad, anxious, and pleased. Most people believe that changes in their emotional state are a direct result of the events that they experience. Let's begin to use the symbol A to represent situations that a person experiences and the symbol C to represent the feelings, emotions, and behaviors. This model is described in Figure 4.1.

Often you might notice that there is a relationship between the events that occur and how you feel—you misplace your keys and feel irritable or annoyed; you share a joke with a friend and feel happy. At other times the changes in your emotions might be quite subtle;

**FIGURE 4.1** *A Leads to C*

**A** =

the situation or event experienced

↓

is presumed to lead directly to

↓

**C** =

feelings, emotions, and behaviors

Think of the As that you have experienced so far today. Perhaps you could write them down:

_____

_____

_____

_____

_____

_____

Now for each situation (A) that you might have experienced, describe how the situation/ event made you feel (C):

_____

_____

_____

_____

_____

_____

_____

you might notice a change in your mood, but it might be difficult to identify any precise cause. The importance of the cognitive theory is that it suggests that, in such situations, people should examine their thoughts to find the clue to their emotions.

On any ordinary day you may not experience any significant events, such as winning the lottery or obtaining a speeding fine. However, any event that does occur during the day may trigger some change in your emotional state. At times, you might find that you experience stronger emotional reactions to a particular situation or event on one occasion, compared to another. For example, one day you might notice feeling very angry that you have misplaced your keys, and on another occasion this same event might not bother you very much. It is also often the case that you may find that some situations or events that didn't bother you will provoke strong emotional reactions in another person.

How can these variations be explained? The cognitive theory of emotions asserts that the influence of an event or situation on a person's feelings, emotions, and behavior is through the way in which the person thinks in response to each event that he or she experiences. Thus, any event that you experience during the day may trigger some spontaneous or *automatic thoughts* (words, sentences, self-statements, or mental images) that, in turn, will produce some change in your emotional state.

During every waking moment you will experience a constant stream of thoughts running through your mind. These thoughts we will refer to as *automatic thoughts*. They can be considered as falling into three main categories: neutral, positive, and negative.

1. *Neutral automatic thoughts* are unlikely to have any significant effect on your emotions, feelings, or behavior (e.g., "Which CD will I listen to?" "What will I eat for lunch?").
2. *Negative automatic thoughts* are likely to have negative, pessimistic, or distressing effects on your emotions, feelings, and behavior (e.g., "I can't cope," "I'm hopeless," "What a mess"). Such thoughts can make you feel anxious, uncertain, inadequate, frustrated, and miserable, among other negative emo-

tional states. Initial negative thoughts may give rise to other thoughts, which, in turn, escalate in negativity. It might be difficult to stop such negative thoughts, and the negative emotional state they produce may deepen.

**3.** *Positive automatic thoughts* are likely to have a positive, optimistic, or comforting effect on your emotions, feelings, and behavior (e.g., "I've done a great job," "I enjoyed that movie," "I can do it"). Such thoughts can make you feel happy, confident, capable, self-assured, in control, and so on.

The model described in Figure 4.1, which holds that A leads to C, fails to take into account the nature of the thoughts (including beliefs, perceptions, and expectations) that a person might hold in reaction to any situation or event that he or she experiences. The cognitive theory asserts that thoughts, let's refer to these as B, intervene between points A and C. The A-B-C model is described in Figure 4.2.

**FIGURE 4.2** *The A-B-C Model*

---

**A =**

the situation or event a person experiences

leads to

↓

**B =**

the thoughts, beliefs, perceptions, and expectations about the situation (A)

and produces

↓

**C =**

a person's feelings, emotions, and behaviors

---

## *The A-B-C Model*

The purpose of the A-B-C model is to illustrate the relationship between situations and events you experience, your thoughts, and your emotional reactions. In particular, A refers to the situation or event you experience; B refers to your thoughts, beliefs, perceptions, and expectations you might have about the situation (A); and C refers to your emotional state. It is important to recognize that the letters *A, B,* and *C* are merely symbols with no specific meaning other than the shorthand code for explaining the relationship between thoughts and emotions, which is based on the cognitive theory of emotions.

Let's consider one general example of the A-B-C model described in Figure 4.3. In this example, the situation (A) is that a person is waiting for a friend who is running a half-hour late.

The important thing to note in this example is that the situation or event at (A) remains identical, but the emotional consequence (C) differs according to the content of the thoughts at B. The main point here is that, according to the cognitive theory of emotions, the emotional consequence (C) is the result of the content of the thoughts (B), *not the event itself* (A). Given the nature of the situation (waiting for a friend who is running late), there might be several positive and negative responses to this event. The same

**FIGURE 4.3**   *The A-B-C Model: A General Example*

| A = The Situation or Event | B = Thoughts and Beliefs | C = Emotional Consequence |
|---|---|---|
| Waiting for a friend who is half an hour late | "She doesn't care; if she did she would be on time." | Neglected, Depressed |
| Waiting for a friend who is half an hour late | "I can't wait to see her!" | Excited, Happy |
| Waiting for a friend who is half an hour late | "I hope nothing has happened." | Anxious, Concerned |
| Waiting for a friend who is half an hour late | "She's always late." | Accepting, Tolerant |

principles that apply to negative emotional states also apply to positive emotional states. That is, happy moods may be the result of positive or constructive thoughts about daily events.

## *Self-Assessment Exercise 6: Practicing the A-B-C Model*

Have a look at the exercises provided in Figure 4.4. In the first exercise you are provided with a description of a situation (A) and some likely thoughts in response to the situation (B). Try to identify some

**FIGURE 4.4** *Self-Assessment Exercise 6: The A-B-C Model*

**Exercise 1:** Complete Column C

| A = The Situation or Event | B = Thoughts and Beliefs | C = Emotional Consequence |
|---|---|---|
| Running late for an appointment | "I'm hopeless!" | _____ |
| Running late for an appointment | "I didn't cause the traffic jam!" | _____ |
| Running late for an appointment | "It's not the end of the world!" | _____ |
| Running late for an appointment | "I never do anything right!" | _____ |

**Exercise 2:** Complete Column B

| A = The Situation or Event | B = Thoughts and Beliefs | C = Emotional Consequence |
|---|---|---|
| Misplacing your keys | _____ _____ | Acceptance, Unconcerned |
| Misplacing your keys | _____ _____ | Angry, Furious |
| Misplacing your keys | _____ _____ | Hopeless, Stupid |
| Misplacing your keys | _____ _____ | Worried, Fearful |

*Continued*

**FIGURE 3.4** *Continued*

---

**Exercise 3:** Identify Two Positive and Two Negative Thoughts at B, and Their Likely Emotional Consequences at C

| A = The Situation or Event | B = Thoughts and Beliefs | C = Emotional Consequence |
|---|---|---|
| Waiting in a queue | _____ _____ | _____ _____ |
| Waiting in a queue | _____ _____ | _____ _____ |
| Waiting in a queue | _____ _____ | _____ _____ |
| Waiting in a queue | _____ _____ | _____ _____ |

**Exercise 4:** Identify Two Positive and Two Negative Thoughts at B, and Their Likely Emotional Consequences at C

| A = The Situation or Event | B = Thoughts and Beliefs | C = Emotional Consequence |
|---|---|---|
| Being complimented at work | _____ _____ | _____ _____ |
| Being complimented at work | _____ _____ | _____ _____ |
| Being complimented at work | _____ _____ | _____ _____ |
| Being complimented at work | _____ _____ | _____ _____ |

---

of the possible emotional consequences and complete column C. In the second exercise, again a situation is described (A), and some potential emotional consequences (C). This time try to identify some possible thoughts (both positive/constructive and negative ones) in column B. In the third and fourth exercises you are provided with a description of a situation (A). Now try to provide examples of two potentially positive and two negative thoughts (B) and their likely emotional effects (C). Notice that the fourth exercise describes a potentially positive situation (being complimented at work) but it is possible to think in a negative way even in response to such situations.

## Extending the A-B-C Model to Understanding Reactions to Tinnitus

The explanation for understanding emotional reactions to events that you might experience in your daily life (i.e., the cognitive theory of emotions, or the A-B-C model) can be expanded to deal with the problem of tinnitus. Let's consider the way in which people think about *sounds* in general. Most people hear sounds as part of their everyday routine—for example, the sound of birds in the trees, traffic, television, radio, wind, garbage trucks, heavy machinery, construction work, sirens, electric fans, computers, music, conversations, or laughter. People often do not notice the sounds until they focus on them. Perhaps attention is drawn to the sounds because they have changed in some way, because someone mentions the sound, or because they have a special meaning (e.g., hearing your own name in a din of conversation at a party or being called by a friend).

## Self-Assessment Exercise 7: Applying the A-B-C Model to Sounds

Now try the exercise described in Figure 4.5. Just imagine the situation (A) that you hear a loud sound in the night.

- What might you think in response to this situation (B)?
- How would you feel (C)?

In Figure 4.5 we provide some examples of some potential thoughts in response to this situation (A) and some possible emo-

**FIGURE 4.5**   *Self-Assessment Exercise 7: Applying the A-B-C Model to Sounds*

| A = The Situation or Event | B = Thoughts and Beliefs | C = Emotional Consequence |
|---|---|---|
| Hearing a loud sound in the night | "There is a burglar in the house!" | Fear, Anxiety |
| Hearing a loud sound in the night | "I must have left the gate open again." | Anger, Irritation |
| Hearing a loud sound in the night | "It's the dog again!" | Annoyed |
| Hearing a loud sound in the night | "It's just the wind." | Neutral |
| Hearing a loud sound in the night | _____ | _____ |
| Hearing a loud sound in the night | _____ | _____ |

tional consequences. Again, it is important to recognize that in this example the situation (A) remains the same, but depending on the content of the thoughts at B, a different emotional consequence arises at C. Try to come up with two of your own examples, one that describes a negative emotional consequence and one that describes a positive emotional consequence.

Any situation or event that a person experiences (A), including a sound, may lead to some thought (self-statement) (B), which, in turn, may produce some emotional response (C), depending on the content of the thought (B). Tinnitus can also be viewed as a sound (A) to which a person can respond in different ways, especially when it varies in loudness or other characteristics. Read through the tinnitus-related examples of the A-B-C model described in Figure 4.6.

As you read through these tinnitus-specific examples, notice that the situation (A) remains identical, but depending on the content of the thoughts at B, a differing emotional consequence (C) is produced. It is not the situation (A) that a person is exposed to that

**FIGURE 4.6** *Tinnitus-Related Examples of the A-B-C Model*

**Example 1:**

| A = The Situation or Event | B = Thoughts and Beliefs | C = Emotional Consequence |
|---|---|---|
| Having tinnitus | "Why me? What did I do to deserve this?" | Frustration, Despair |
| Having tinnitus | "The sound drives me crazy!" | Helplessness, Depression |
| Having tinnitus | "I can control it." | Self-assured, Confident |
| Having tinnitus | "I just can't cope." | Hopeless, Miserable |
| Having tinnitus | "The noise is not pleasant but I can cope with it!" | Hopeful, In control |
| Having tinnitus | "The noise is a nuisance, but there are so many things in life I enjoy!" | Optimistic, Acceptance |

**Example 2**

| A = The Situation or Event | B = Thoughts and Beliefs | C = Emotional Consequence |
|---|---|---|
| Invited to a party | "It will make my tinnitus worse." | Despair, Hopeless |
| Invited to a party | "It will be noisy and I won't hear what is being said." | Frustration, Tension |
| Invited to a party | "I hate noisy places!" | Annoyance |
| Invited to a party | "That will take my mind off my tinnitus." | Excited, Hopeful |
| Invited to a party | "My tinnitus might be a bit of a bother, but I can still enjoy the function." | Optimistic, Acceptance |
| Invited to a party | "Being in a noisy place makes my tinnitus a bit louder, but it will settle." | Reassured, Positive |

leads to how he or she feels (C). More importantly, it is what the person thinks to himself or herself (B) that has a powerful influence on the person's emotions and feelings (C). As portrayed in Figure 4.7, tinnitus can be regarded as an event (A) to which a person may respond with thoughts or self-statements or beliefs (B), which, in turn, may lead to some emotional state (C).

## *Characteristics of Automatic Thoughts*

There are a number of characteristics of automatic thoughts that we would like to highlight. Automatic thoughts (1) seem to arise with little awareness, (2) are highly believable, and (3) appear to be out of direct control. That is, people are often unaware of the content of their thoughts unless there is an opportunity to pause and attend to them. People can be influenced by the content to have a certain emotional response without necessarily being aware of the content itself. They also tend to believe their thoughts without questioning the basis of such thoughts. Of course, people believe their own

**FIGURE 4.7**   *The A-B-C Model Applied to Tinnitus*

---

**A =**

situation: having tinnitus

leads to

↓

**B =**

your thoughts, beliefs, perceptions, and expectations about having tinnitus

and produces

↓

**C =**

your emotions, feelings, and behavior in response to your tinnitus

---

thoughts and do not normally question their personal ways of thinking. Their thoughts are their reality. However, it would be surprising if everyone's thoughts were accurate perceptions of an event! You might be able to recall times when you have had a particular thought about an event, only to discover later that it was not correct. Sometimes, thoughts are accurate, and on other occasions, they may be partly or wholly in error. Perhaps you can remember a particular event (e.g., a remark made by a friend) and the emotion that you felt (e.g., upset), but not the thoughts that were going through your mind at the time (e.g., "He said that deliberately to hurt me!"). The emotion stays with a person but the thought evaporates like the content of his or her dreams. Often, one thought will tend to trigger off another thought of the same type. The process can become a bit like a *broken record* repeating the same sequences. That is, one negative or unhelpful thought can lead to a series of such thoughts and with each thought there may be a deepening of negative emotional states.

## *Self-Assessment Exercise 8: What Are the Effects of Negative Automatic Thoughts?*

In order for you to begin to understand some of the effects of negative thoughts on your reactions to tinnitus, consider the practical exercise that we describe in Figure 4.8. We list some examples of common thoughts about tinnitus that people have described in some of our groups. Read through the examples and then consider some of the possible emotional consequences of thinking such thoughts.

Some possible emotions that you might have identified in response to the exercise depicted in Figure 4.8 may include feeling hopeless, helpless, angry, miserable, depressed, frustrated, and distressed. It is understandable that a person who has to endure the constant sound of tinnitus might engage in such negative kinds of thoughts. However, this style of thinking in response to tinnitus can simply compound the problem by producing:

**FIGURE 4.8** *Self-Assessment Exercise 8:*
*Effects of Negative Thoughts*

From our own clinical experience some examples of common thoughts that people report in response to tinnitus (A) include:

*B = Thoughts*

1. "Why me? Why do I have to suffer this noise?"
2. "I just can't cope with this sound!"
3. "The buzzing noise ruins everything for me!"
4. "This is not fair—the noise will drive me crazy!"
5. "Before I developed tinnitus everything was fine—now things are terrible!"
6. "My tinnitus is getting louder!"
7. "I can't bear it!"

Take a moment to consider the emotional consequences of a person thinking these thoughts in response to having tinnitus. If you were to think these thoughts how might you feel?

*C = Emotions*

1. _____
2. _____
3. _____
4. _____
5. _____
6. _____
7. _____

- Negative and distressing emotional consequences (e.g., feelings of despair, frustration, anger, irritability, depression, etc.).
- A vicious cycle: Negative thoughts about tinnitus can lead to negative emotions and greater focus of attention on tinnitus, which gives rise to further negative thoughts, greater distress, and so on.
- A state wherein you may become "absorbed" by the problem of having tinnitus. Many people with tinnitus report that when their tinnitus is particularly bothersome, they find they are

more aware of it, and they have difficulty directing their attention to anything else. Research on chronic pain indicates that focusing attention on pain heightens the pain and associated distress. This is likely to be true with tinnitus.

- Avoidance of social, leisure, and work commitments, or other activities that might usually provide a sense of fulfillment, achievement, and pleasure. This results in restrictions and disruptions to daily routine and lifestyle. It also allows for little opportunity to be distracted from the tinnitus.
- A reduction in your ability to cope effectively with tinnitus.

## Changing the Way You Think in Response to Your Tinnitus

Negative thinking in response to your tinnitus can produce detrimental effects on your emotions, behavior, and psychological well-being. If you have a tendency to think in a negative manner, particularly with regard to your tinnitus, then this destructive process produced by the negative thinking can be reversed by *learning to change the content of your thoughts* in response to your tinnitus. The tinnitus may still be present, but you can learn ways to react differently to the problem.

To learn to think in a constructive way in response to your tinnitus, there are seven essential steps that you need to follow:

1. Acknowledge the impact of your thoughts about yourself and the situations or events that you experience, on your feelings, emotions, and behavior.
2. Deliberately tune in and listen to what you are saying or thinking to yourself, particularly when feeling either (a) strong negative emotions, such as anger or sadness, or (b) strong positive emotions, such as excitement or happiness.
3. Identify positive, constructive, or neutral thoughts. These thoughts will have positive or neutral effects on your thoughts and feelings.

4. Identify negative, unhelpful thoughts—these will have negative effects on your feelings and emotions.

5. Interrupt and stop negative thoughts. By doing this you can avoid allowing your thoughts to operate like a broken record, continuing on and on.

6. Challenge the truth and validity of your thoughts—do not blindly accept negative automatic thoughts as true.

7. Substitute constructive counterthoughts for every identified (and challenged) unrealistic or unhelpful thought.

## *Self-Assessment Exercise 9: Becoming Aware of the Content of Your Thoughts*

The purpose of this exercise is to help you begin the process of cognitive therapy (i.e., described in the preceding seven points). This exercise will help you practice points 1 to 4: acknowledging the relationship between thoughts and emotions, becoming aware of the content of your thoughts, and learning to identify negative automatic thoughts. In Figure 4.9 we provide you with a recording form for you to complete. Read through the instructions and then begin to monitor the content of your thoughts on a daily basis. By doing so, you will have taken the first steps in learning to change the way you think in response to your tinnitus. In the next chapter we will instruct you in some other cognitive (thought-management) techniques to help you to manage your tinnitus.

## *Conclusion*

In this chapter we have described the cognitive theory of emotion and the ABC model to illustrate the powerful relationship that exists between situations and events you experience, your thoughts, and your emotional reactions. It is not uncommon for people to respond to their tinnitus by engaging in negative styles of thinking, such as, "Why me?" "This sound will drive me crazy," and "I can't stand this noise." These negative thoughts may give rise to

**FIGURE 4.9** *Self-Assessment Exercise 9:*
*Monitoring Your Thoughts*

The A-B-C model describes the important relationship between events, thoughts, and emotions. This monitoring form is designed to assist you in learning to identify negative automatic thoughts that you might think in response to your tinnitus or to other stressful events. In column A briefly describe the situation that you experienced; in column B write down the thoughts that you have identified; and in column C describe the emotions that you felt. You can use this form to monitor your progress in learning to identify negative thoughts and to highlight the powerful relationship between your thoughts and emotions.

| Date | A = Situation | B = Thoughts | C = Emotions |
|------|---------------|--------------|--------------|
| Example | Unable to sleep because of loud tinnitus | I can't stand it. This is unbearable. | Frustrated, Hopeless, Depressed, Helpless |
|  |  |  |  |
|  |  |  |  |
|  |  |  |  |
|  |  |  |  |
|  |  |  |  |

distressing emotions, including feelings of despair, frustration, and depression. You can alleviate these negative emotional states by learning to change the content of your thoughts in response to your tinnitus. The tinnitus may still be present, but you can learn effective ways to react differently to the problem.

# 5

## *Changing the Way You Think about Tinnitus*

*Every day of my life I am plagued by the noises in my head. Not one day goes by without it. I hate it. I used to be perfectly healthy, not a thing wrong with me. When my tinnitus is really bad I just feel sick. Life used to be great, but the constant noise has ruined it for me. Nothing will ever be the same. I just get so angry and frustrated. Even on a good day, I don't enjoy things like I used to. I keep asking why this had to happen? Why me? What did I do to deserve this? Anything would be better than having to put up with this noise! There is nothing, nothing, that could possibly be this bad. I might have had a few problems in the past, but this has got to be the worst thing that I have ever had to endure!*

In Chapter 4 we looked at how the thoughts, beliefs, and expectations that a person holds in response to their tinnitus may have a powerful influence on their emotions, feelings, and behavior. Automatic thoughts may essentially be classified as positive, negative, or neutral. *Positive thoughts* tend to have the effect of making a person feel good and optimistic. *Neutral thoughts* usually have no significant effect on a person's feelings or emotions. *Negative thoughts,* of course, generally have some detrimental effect on a person's feelings, mood, and emotions. It is not uncommon for people to tend to engage in particular patterns or styles of thinking. In the first part of this chapter, we will describe 12 common styles of negative thinking. We will then describe thought-stopping and distraction techniques that can be used to control negative automatic thoughts. In the final section of this chapter, we will introduce you to an approach called *cognitive restructuring*.

## The 12 Common Styles of Negative Thinking*

### 1. *Overgeneralization*
You come to a general conclusion on the basis of a single piece of evidence. If something bad happened once, you expect it to happen over and over again.

| **General Example** | **Tinnitus Example** |
| --- | --- |
| I failed to score a goal in the game. I never will. | Because of my tinnitus I was awake all night. Every night will be the same. |

### 2. *All-or-None Thinking*
You see things in distinct categories—black or white. Things are good or bad, perfect or a failure. There are no shades of grey.

| **General Example** | **Tinnitus Example** |
| --- | --- |
| I've lost my job—now everything is a disaster. | Before I had tinnitus my life was perfect. Now, my life is ruined. |

### 3. *Filtering*
You tend to select a single negative event, filter out all positive features, and dwell on the negative exclusively.

| **General Example** | **Tinnitus Example** |
| --- | --- |
| No one finished the dessert—the rest of the food seemed popular, but the dessert ruined the whole evening. | My tinnitus is much worse after the party—I enjoyed the company but my tinnitus spoiled everything. |

*List adapted from Henry & Wilson (2001).

**4.** *Mind Reading or Jumping to Conclusions*
You know what people are feeling and why they act the way they do, even without them saying so or without asking them.

| *General Example* | *Tinnitus Example* |
|---|---|
| I know that my friends all hate me because I forgot to book the table at the restaurant. | When I have to ask people to repeat things because I don't hear well, I know they think I'm an idiot. |

**5.** *Magnification or Catastrophizing*
You expect the worst and make mountains out of molehills.

| *General Example* | *Tinnitus Example* |
|---|---|
| I'll make a fool of myself and then I'll never be able to show my face in public. | My tinnitus is louder—I know I'll become deaf. |

**6.** *Minimization*
You tend to belittle the importance of the significance of an event, or even your own strengths or assets.

| *General Example* | *Tinnitus Example* |
|---|---|
| So what if I'm a good cook? That doesn't mean anything. | So what if I managed my tinnitus today? That was a fluke. |

**7.** *Personalization*
You tend to blame yourself inappropriately as the cause of a negative event.

| *General Example* | *Tinnitus Example* |
|---|---|
| That disagreement was all my fault. | I was so annoyed by my tinnitus that I ruined the night for everyone. |

**8.** *Jumping to Conclusions*
You tend to draw a conclusion despite the fact that the evidence is lacking or actually supports the contrary conclusion.

| *General Example* | *Tinnitus Example* |
|---|---|
| The boss might say I've done a good job and the figures show it, but I know I haven't. | The tests say that my hearing is O.K., but I know I'm going deaf. |

**9.** *Emotional Reasoning*
You believe that whatever you feel must be true—automatically. You assume that if you feel negative, then this feeling is an accurate reflection of the way things really are.

| *General Example* | *Tinnitus Example* |
|---|---|
| I feel stupid—I am stupid. | My tinnitus makes me feel so hopeless. There is no hope. |

**10.** *"Should" Statements*
You have an ironclad list of rules about how you and others "should" behave. If others break these rules, you feel angry; if you break them, you experience guilt.

| *General Example* | *Tinnitus Example* |
|---|---|
| I should always be happy. | Having tinnitus should never upset me. |

**11.** *Labeling*
You tend to generalize one or two qualities into a negative global judgment. (This is an extreme form of overgeneralization.)

| *General Example* | *Tinnitus Example* |
|---|---|
| I made a mistake. I'm a total loser, a hopeless case. | Having tinnitus and hearing loss means that I'm totally disabled. |

**12.** *Blaming*
You hold other people responsible for all of your troubles, or, alternatively, you blame yourself for everyone else's troubles.

| *General Example* | *Tinnitus Example* |
|---|---|
| If it hadn't been for my partner hassling me, I would have done O.K. | I wouldn't be so annoyed with my tinnitus if my family understood! |

## *Learning to Control Negative Thinking*

So far we have looked at the powerful influence of thoughts on a person's emotions and behavior. We have also discussed some common styles of negative thinking. As we explained in Chapter 4, thoughts are usually fairly automatic. That is, they are part of a spontaneous and constant stream of thoughts that run through a person's mind throughout the day. Because they are so familiar and habitual, they tend to be believable. Not only are thoughts fairly automatic, but one thought can trigger off another similar thought. Thoughts and "self-talk" can become just like a broken record, going on and on and on. One negative thought can lead to another, which can lead to another, and so on.

In Chapter 4 we introduced you to the process of monitoring the content of your thoughts in order to increase your ability to identify negative automatic thoughts as soon as you become aware of them. A further important skill involved in learning to think in a rational and constructive manner is to learn to interrupt and stop these thoughts once they are identified. It might be useful to imagine that your thoughts are like having a cassette player in your head constantly switched to "play." Imagine that the cassette is playing, your thoughts are flowing constantly, then you become aware of a negative thought. Instead of allowing this to trigger another negative thought, you need to learn to press the "pause" button. This will give you time to pause and to prevent a potentially destructive flow of negative thoughts. Once you have interrupted a negative thought, it is important that you then refocus your attention onto some neutral or positive thought by using a distraction method (which will be described in the following section).

A number of techniques are available that are helpful in learning to interrupt and control negative thinking. In the following section, we describe three specific techniques that have proven to be useful in learning to control one's negative thoughts. These techniques include thought-stopping strategies, distraction methods, and increasing positive thoughts. We will begin by describing a number of thought-stopping strategies that can help you to learn how to switch on the "pause" button. We recommend that you work through these techniques, practicing each one for a reasonable period of time, such as every day for a week or two. This daily practice will help you determine which of the techniques works best for you. Consistent and regular practice will strengthen your skill in using them to control negative thoughts in your response to tinni-

tus. In time, you will become more confident in your ability to identify and stop negative thoughts and you will develop a greater sense
of control over your thoughts.

## Thought-Stopping Techniques

When you notice that you are thinking a negative thought, immediately use one of the following thought-stopping techniques:

- Say to yourself: "I am going to stop thinking about that now!"
- Imagine as vividly as possible a large red stop sign. Follow its
  signal and stop thinking the negative thought.
- Mentally "shout" the word *stop* without making a sound, but
  feel the full force just as if you were actually shouting. Should
  you find this difficult, it might be useful to begin practicing this
  technique in private (e.g., at home alone). First, start to think
  some negative thought. As soon as you notice the thought,
  shout the word *stop* as loudly as you can. Repeat this process
  over several days but begin to gradually reduce the volume of
  your "shouting" until you can mentally "shout" *stop* without
  making a sound, but feeling the full force. Obviously, now you
  can begin to use this technique in public.
- Wear a heavy-gauge rubber band around your wrist. As soon as
  you notice a negative thought, snap the band against your
  wrist.
- Take a deep breath in, mentally think the word *one*. Then,
  while breathing out, mentally think the word *relax* and relax
  all your muscles. Continue the process, repeating the two
  words at least 10 times.

## Distraction Methods

Immediately after you have interrupted a negative thought using
a thought-stopping technique, it is important to refocus your
thoughts onto something nonnegative. Otherwise, you might find
that you simply focus back onto the previous negative thought.
Listed here are some suggested distraction exercises. These will

assist you in achieving some relief from negative thinking, lessening any emotional distress, and promoting a greater sense of control over your thoughts. Remember, the process of learning to control negative automatic thoughts involves several steps:

1. Recognize the powerful relationship between thoughts and emotions.
2. Become aware of the content of your thoughts.
3. Identify negative automatic thoughts as soon as they arise.
4. Use thought-stopping techniques to interrupt the flow of negative thoughts.
5. Use distraction techniques to allow time for you to pause and reflect on nonnegative or pleasant thoughts.

Practice each of the following distraction methods in order to determine which technique(s) suits you best:

- Mentally count backwards from 100 by 7s.
- Mentally run through the letters of the alphabet backwards (Z through A).
- Mentally run through the months of the year backwards (December through January).
- Mentally run through the words of a favorite song.
- Mentally relive your last holiday.
- Imagine you have won one million dollars in a lottery—how would you spend it?
- Imagine yourself in a favorite place (e.g., at the beach, in the country, fishing, sitting in front of a log fire). Capture a vivid mental image of this place—what can you see, hear, smell, feel, taste?
- Plan a shopping list.
- Plan a menu for a dinner party.
- Think of a movie that you have enjoyed.
- Plan your next holiday.

In Figure 5.1 we present some examples to illustrate how some people have made use of thought-stopping and distraction techniques to help them deal with negative thoughts in response to tinnitus.

**FIGURE 5.1** *Examples to Illustrate the Use of Thought-Stopping Techniques*

---

### Example 1

*My biggest problem with tinnitus is that it disturbs my sleep. I have never been a good sleeper. But now that I have this constant ringing and buzzing in both ears I find it impossible. In the quiet of the night all I can hear is my tinnitus. Often I will toss and turn for hours on end. I will often lie there thinking: "I can't stand this. I have to get some sleep. How will I ever function at work tomorrow? This is awful". Thinking these thoughts just made me more and more upset. I could feel myself getting tense and uptight—I just wanted to scream! I tried a number of things to try to stop my negative thoughts. One thing that does seem to help is that I focus on my breathing. I think the word blue as I breathe in (I've always found the color blue to be relaxing), and then when I breathe out I think the word relax and just focus on letting all of the tension flow out of my muscles. I just keep focusing on relaxing my body. I then pick some number, like 424, or whatever, and mentally I just subtract 7 and slowly count backwards by 7s—I don't bother whether my calculations are correct—and as I count backwards I try to become more deeply relaxed. I do find this helps not thinking about anything else, such as my tinnitus. The more I practice this, the easier it's getting.*

### Example 2

*I thought the idea of snapping a rubber band against my wrist was a bit silly when I first heard it. But I thought I'd try it. See, I'm wearing one now! I find that if I'm tired or under some sort of stress I am more likely to think very negatively. The first time I used the band was one day when I had been very busy at work. I was tired and I had to go to the movies that night with a friend. I often find the noise at the movies so loud! I was worrying that my tinnitus would be worse when I got home afterwards. When I first noticed myself thinking about this I "slapped" the band against my wrist. Well, that made me forget about*

**FIGURE 5.1** *Continued*

---

*those worries! Then I spent a few moments thinking about how good it would be to catch up with my friend. I've used the rubber band a few times since, but I have actually found that wearing the band and just the sight of it on my wrist helps me to be more aware of the thoughts that are running through my mind. I seem to notice them earlier. I think this is just to help me stop the thought sooner. Then I don't have to use it—I just distract myself by focusing on some positive aspect of whatever situation I find myself in. Maybe I'm cheating—but I am beginning to feel more in control of my thoughts. I am often asked why I have a rubber band around my wrist! However, this doesn't bother me at all—in fact it only reminds me how far I have come in regaining control over my tinnitus.*

---

## Tipping the Balance: How to Increase Positive Thoughts

People often tend to focus on negative aspects of their lives (e.g., their personal shortcomings, failures, tinnitus, etc.) and ignore the positive aspects (e.g., their achievements, successes, family, friends, pleasurable hobbies, etc.). Another way of learning to manage negative thinking is to use techniques that will increase the frequency of positive thinking. Here are some suggestions to try.

**1.** Focus less on those personal factors that you consider to be negative and begin to focus more on your positive or good points. First, you need to put together a list of positive thoughts about yourself. If you have difficulty, then ask people whom you trust to tell you what they consider to be your good points. Write these thoughts down on small sheets of paper, one thought per page. Arrange these pages in a pack—just like a pack of cards. Carry them with you each day in your wallet, pocket, bag, or even in the glove box of your car. At random intervals throughout each day, take out your pack of positive thoughts, pull out one sheet, and read the thought and pay serious attention to it. Add new thoughts to the pack as they occur to you. Also, begin to place "wild cards" within your pack—that is, a blank sheet of paper. When you pull out a blank sheet (i.e., a "wild-card"), come up with a new/additional positive thought about your-self on the spot!

**2.** You can increase the frequency of positive thoughts by pair-ing them with things that you do frequently. Use frequent behav-iors, or activities, as reminders to think a positive thought. For example, remind yourself to think a positive thought each time you eat, brush your teeth, use the telephone, read something, get in and out of your car, use public transportation, and so on.

## How to Challenge Negative Automatic Thoughts: The Process of Cognitive Restructuring

In Chapter 4 we discussed some of the characteristics of automatic thoughts, such as the way in which they tend to be highly believ-able. People usually believe their thoughts without questioning their basis. However, it would be rather surprising if all of a person's thoughts were accurate perceptions of events he or she experiences! Sometimes, thoughts are accurate, and, on other occasions, they may be partly or wholly in error. To illustrate this feature of auto-matic thoughts, let's consider a general example of the A-B-C model that is described in Figure 5.2.

In the example presented in Figure 5.2, the person who is hav-ing trouble with the bank machine probably has no real evidence that the individual who has offered assistance thinks that the per-son in need of help is stupid. Nor is it likely to be true that all people can readily use the bank machines without assistance. Indeed, many people avoid these machines altogether for fear of making a mistake in front of other people. Thus, in this example there are two aspects of the thought that are probably erroneous: (1) an example of reading another person's mind—thinking that you know accu-rately what another person is thinking and (2) an example of a false comparison—assuming that you are unique in not possessing cer-tain skills. At a deeper level, these thoughts may also suggest that

**FIGURE 5.2**　*A General Example of the A-B-C Model*

| A = The Situation or Event | B = Thoughts and Beliefs | C = Emotional Consequence |
| --- | --- | --- |
| Offer of help with automatic bank machine | "It is reassuring to know that there are helpful people around when I need them." | Positive, Pleasure |
| Offer of help with automatic bank machine | "I feel like such an idiot that I cannot use this machine. This person must think that I am really stupid. Everyone else can use these machines." | Depressed, Hopeless |

the person holds a high degree of concern about what other people think, or how important it is to be able to perform tasks correctly and independently.

The danger of simply accepting negative thoughts as accurate and believable is that a person may place a high degree of certainty in his or her thoughts. This may lead to more negative thoughts, and these thoughts may become automatic, familiar, and believable. As a consequence, a person may experience negative feelings and emotions. If a person thinks "I'm hopeless and worthless" that person is likely to begin to *feel* hopeless and worthless. He or she may then take these feelings as confirmation and evidence that his or her thoughts are true. This may easily lead to a vicious circle and a pattern of circular reasoning, as described in Figure 5.3.

The next important skill for you to learn is *how to challenge or question your thoughts*. This involves seeking concrete evidence to prove that your thinking is *valid, correct, and in perspective*. Once you have challenged your thoughts, and if you find them to be incorrect, faulty, unrealistic, and out of perspective, you need to substitute some more correct, reasonable, and realistic thoughts in their place. These counterthoughts should be *brief, easily remembered, believable, realistic, and personally relevant*. Through the process of challenging negative and unhelpful thoughts, you can learn to think in a more constructive and helpful way.

**FIGURE 5.3   *A Circular Pattern of Reasoning***

---

"I am hopeless and worthless!"

↓

"I feel hopeless and worthless!"

↓

"I must be hopeless and worthless—a total loser!"

---

Constructive thinking is not simply a matter of positive thinking. Positive thinking, such as, "I'm great; everything is wonderful; I won't be bothered by my tinnitus at all" may not be that helpful because these thoughts might not be realistic or believable even to yourself. Rather, constructive thinking involves looking at the facts of a situation realistically and ensuring that your thoughts in response to an event or situation are not distorted by hasty or incorrect exaggerations and catastrophizing (refer back to the common styles of negative thinking described at the beginning of this chapter).

## *The A-B-C-D-E Model*

We will now introduce two further steps to the A-B-C model:

1. **D** = disputing or challenging unrealistic, unhelpful thoughts, self-talk, or beliefs (contained in B)
2. **E** = new emotional consequence(s); that is, a different emotional consequence is produced by replacing negative automatic thoughts at B with constructive thoughts (at D)

Thus, the A-B-C model now becomes the A-B-C-D-E model that is described in Figure 5.4.

**FIGURE 5.4** *The A-B-C-D-E Model*

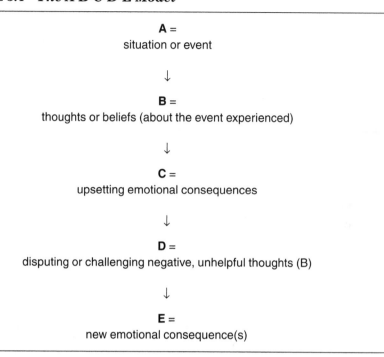

**A =**
situation or event

↓

**B =**
thoughts or beliefs (about the event experienced)

↓

**C =**
upsetting emotional consequences

↓

**D =**
disputing or challenging negative, unhelpful thoughts (B)

↓

**E =**
new emotional consequence(s)

## *Guidelines for Challenging Your Thoughts*

In order to challenge negative thoughts, you need to examine your thoughts and test them against whatever evidence you have to determine how valid or accurate they are. This process, called *cognitive restructuring,* involves asking yourself a series of questions to explore whether the available evidence supports the content of your thoughts. To help you to do this, here are some questions that you might ask yourself:

1. What is actually true about this situation?
2. What is the evidence that my thinking is true and correct?
3. What facts am I forgetting or ignoring?

4. What distortions or mistakes am I making in my thinking? (Read through "The 12 Common Styles of Negative Thinking" at the beginning of this chapter.)
5. What is *not* true about this situation?
6. What are the facts, and what am I making up or exaggerating?
7. What are some other ways of thinking about this situation?
8. Have I considered all other possible thoughts and explanations?
9. Is there a more positive way of looking at this situation?
10. Is there anything good about this situation?
11. What other practical things could I do to deal with this situation?
12. What else could I do in this situation?
13. Is the situation as bad as I am making it out to be?
14. What is the worst thing that could happen?
15. How likely is it that the worst thing will happen?
16. How awful is the worst thing should it happen?
17. What is probably, or most likely, going to happen?

For every identified negative automatic thought, it is important to challenge the validity of the thought as soon as you become aware of it. Once you have challenged the thought and found it to be an inaccurate or unhelpful way of thinking, then it is important to substitute more accurate, constructive, or helpful thoughts. Remember, these thoughts should be brief, easily remembered, believable, realistic, and personally relevant. To begin to practice the process of challenging negative thoughts, complete the exercise in Figure 5.5. In this exercise, John is having trouble getting to sleep. We describe his thoughts at B and his emotions at C. Try to come up with some ways to apply the A-B-C-D-E model to John's thoughts (i.e., How could John challenge his negative automatic thoughts?).

**FIGURE 5.5** *Practice in Challenging Negative Automatic Thoughts*

---

### Exercise 1

**A** = *Situation:* John is having trouble getting to sleep.

**B** = This is what John is *thinking* to himself:

> *"The tinnitus is so loud—a constant buzzing! I bet I'll have difficulty getting a good night's sleep. How am I going to function tomorrow? I'll be so tired and irritable. The tinnitus will drive me crazy. I feel so helpless. The sound ruins everything."*

**C** = This is how he is *feeling:*

Helpless, despondent, depressed, irritable, and annoyed

**D** = *Challenging negative, unhelpful thoughts* (B)
- How might John challenge his negative automatic thoughts?
  (What questions might he ask himself to challenge his thoughts?)
  Example: "What are the facts? What am I making up or exaggerating?"

_____

_____

_____

_____

- What might be another way that John could respond to this situation?
  Example: "I'll stop focusing on my tinnitus now, and divert my attention to something pleasant, until I finally drift off to sleep—let's see, I will start thinking and making plans for my next holiday."

_____

_____

_____

_____

_____

*Continued*

**FIGURE 5.5**   *Continued*

- What are some more constructive or helpful thoughts that John might think?
  Example: "In the past, I have managed to get a good night's sleep once I have
  finally drifted off to sleep—so there is no point in catastrophizing now. This will
  only unnecessarily stimulate my mind further."

_____

_____

_____

_____

_____

_____

**E** =   *New emotional consequences*

- If John was to substitute the thoughts at D for those at B, what might be the new
  emotional consequences (feelings) that he might experience at E? Example:
  "More relaxed and calm."

_____

_____

_____

_____

# Self-Assessment Exercise 10: Practicing the A-B-C-D-E Model

To provide you with further practice in the A-B-C-D-E model, complete the self-assessment exercise described in Figure 5.6. In the
first exercise, we present some examples of what some people have
said when they have attempted to think about their tinnitus in a

**FIGURE 5.6** *Self-Assessment Exercise 10: Practicing the A-B-C-D-E Model*

---

### Exercise 1

Listed below are examples of what some people with tinnitus have said when they have attempted to think about the tinnitus in a more constructive way. Read each thought and then describe in the space provided *how you might be feeling* if you were to think this thought in response to your tinnitus.

- *"I think of the noise as being in the room—that is, an external noise."*

_____

- *"I used to think that it invaded me from the outside; now I think that it is ME. I have accepted the noise as being a part of me."*

_____

- *"How much of your world are you prepared to give to tinnitus, and how much to other things?"*

_____

- *"I think of tinnitus as my friend."*

_____

- *"Whatever is happening, I can deal with it."*

_____

- *"I am going to conquer this."*

_____

### Exercise 2

Read through each of the tinnitus-related negative thoughts listed below. Then ask yourself the following questions:

- How might you be feeling if you were thinking in this way?
- How could you challenge each of the thoughts?
- What are some more constructive ways of thinking?

*Continued*

**FIGURE 5.6** *Continued*

---

- If you were to substitute some constructive thoughts in response to the negative thoughts, how might your feelings change?

| *Negative Thoughts* | *Constructive/Helpful Thoughts* |
|---|---|
| No one understands what I'm going through with the tinnitus. | _____ _____ |
| My tinnitus is unbearable and it seems like my whole life is full of it. | _____ _____ |
| My tinnitus prevents me from enjoying life. | _____ _____ |
| How can I accept this party invitation? What if my tinnitus gets worse? | _____ _____ |
| Why me? Why do I have to suffer this noise? | _____ _____ |
| My tinnitus seems to be getting louder— soon I won't be able to hear anything. | _____ _____ |
| The tinnitus will drive me crazy! | _____ _____ |
| With this noise my life is terrible. | _____ _____ |
| The noise will overwhelm me! | _____ _____ |
| Why can't anyone help me? | _____ _____ |

---

more constructive way. Read through this exercise and think about how you might be feeling if you were to think these kinds of thoughts. In the second exercise, we present a series of tinnitus-related negative thoughts. Think about how you could challenge each of these thoughts and then try to develop some more constructive counterstatements. Remember to use some of the questions listed under the heading "Guidelines for Challenging Your Thoughts" presented earlier in this chapter. Complete this exercise at your own pace. Afterwards, read through the suggested constructive thoughts presented in Figure 5.7.

**FIGURE 5.7** *Examples of Tinnitus-Related Negative Thoughts and Constructive Counterthoughts*

| Negative Thoughts | Constructive/Helpful Thoughts |
|---|---|
| No one understands what I'm going through with the tinnitus. | There are lots of unpleasant things I don't understand, but I can still provide comfort—and others can do the same for me. |
| My tinnitus is unbearable and it seems like my whole life is full of it. | I might have tinnitus but there are lots of other pleasant things in my life. |
| My tinnitus prevents me from enjoying life. | At times my tinnitus is annoying, but lots of things still give me pleasure. |
| How can I accept this party invitation? What if my tinnitus gets worse? | Going out socially will be a good distraction. |
| Why me? Why do I have to suffer this noise? | No point asking why—get in and start dealing with it! |
| My tinnitus seems to be getting louder—soon I won't be able to hear anything. | There's no evidence that it will become increasingly loud. |
| The tinnitus will drive me crazy! | It is a nuisance but I can take control of my tinnitus. |
| With this noise my life is terrible. | There are lots of other things that make my life enjoyable. |
| The noise will overwhelm me! | If I take an active role I can learn to control this noise. |
| Why can't anyone help me? | Lots of people can help me if I let them—but I must learn to help myself. |

# Self-Assessment Exercise 11: Learning to Challenge Your Negative Thoughts

In Figure 5.8 we present a monitoring form so that you can begin to practice challenging your own negative automatic thoughts. You can use a copy machine to make a number of copies of this form so that you can practice challenging your thoughts and hence learn the skill of cognitive restructuring. Here is how to use this form:

*Figure 5.8  Self-Assessment Exercise 11: Challenging Negative Thoughts (A-B-C-D-E)*

Date: _____

Use this monitoring form to write down the negative thoughts you have identified and how you challenged them using the A-B-C-D-E model.

| Date | Activating Event/ Situation  A | Your Thought or Beliefs about A  B | Emotional Consequences (Feelings)  C | Disputing or Challenging the Negative Beliefs (i.e., Adaptive Thoughts)  D | New Emotional Consequences (Feelings)  E |
|---|---|---|---|---|---|
| E.G. 3 May | Woke in the night feeling bothered by tinnitus. | I'll be exhausted tomorrow. I can't stand this, I want some peace. | Worried, irritable, frustrated, uptight. | I've had 4 hours sleep—it's not great but I can live with it. There is no point in forcing myself to sleep and getting frustrated. I'll take a warm shower and think about something pleasant. | Felt less irritable and bit more relaxed. |

- In *column A,* briefly describe the situation.
- Record any negative automatic thoughts that you identify in *column B.*
- In *column C,* describe how you were feeling.
- Then ask yourself a series of questions and challenge the negative thoughts (in B).
- In *column D,* record some constructive thoughts to challenge the thoughts listed in column B.
- Then describe the new emotional consequences in *column E.*
- Remember to reread the section "Guidelines for Challenging Your Thoughts," which is presented earlier in this chapter.

## *Conclusion*

We have now introduced you to specific cognitive (thought-management) techniques designed to be used to control one's negative thoughts and/or thinking styles. In summary, in order to regain control over your negative thoughts, we strongly encourage you to apply the thought-stopping and distraction techniques presented in this chapter, as well as increasing the frequency of your positive thoughts. We also recommend that you practice on a regular basis the cognitive-restructuring technique (i.e., the A-B-C-D-E model) in order to help you change the way you think about your tinnitus, particularly if you are prone to experiencing pessimistic and negative tinnitus-related thoughts. We would like to emphasize that with regular practice, you will, over time, become proficient in applying these cognitive skills. Furthermore, it is important to keep in mind that you can use these thought-management strategies to deal with any stressful situation you may encounter in your daily life, such as work, family, and social problems or crises.

# 6

# *Relaxation and Stress-Management Techniques*

*Whenever I'm under some form of stress I find that my tinnitus is much worse. It definitely becomes louder. Usually I hear a sound like a whirring, whining noise, with a buzzing in the background. That's what I hear in both my ears. But when I'm feeling stressed, the noise gets louder and more high-pitched. I also notice a piercing shrill sound in my head—like high-tension wire. That is unbearable. It is so painful! I find I get very irritable and quick-tempered. My whole body seems to go rigid in response to the noise. My muscles become tight— like steel rods through my whole body. My head aches with the sound. My whole body aches! On really bad days I have to take the day off work. I try to relax, but it is so hard with the constant noise! It seems as though any form of stress makes things worse—such as when I'm under pressure at work, trying to meet a deadline, or just trying to juggle everything at home. I have too many things to do and not enough time. I feel so out of control—like I'm going to lose the plot! I used to be able to manage stress, but now with the noises in my head, I just can't seem to cope.*

## *Stress and Tinnitus*

Many people with tinnitus report a relationship between their tinnitus and stress. Some people comment that their tinnitus makes them nervous and tense; alternatively, others comment that their tinnitus becomes worse during periods of physical or emotional stress or fatigue. It is possible that the presence of external stress may lead a person to view the tinnitus in a more negative manner, simply because stress makes everything seem worse (including the tinnitus). In order to gauge whether there is a relationship between your tinnitus and stress, here are some questions you might consider:

- Does your tinnitus get louder when you are under stress?
- Do you have more difficulty managing your tinnitus when you are under stress?
- What sort of stress makes it more difficult to manage your tinnitus?

## *What Is Relaxation Training?*

Relaxation training helps a person achieve deep levels of physical relaxation, producing a state of mental calmness and tranquility. Relaxation can also decrease the time that it takes to fall asleep and can improve the quality of sleep. Essentially, relaxation training is a valuable life skill to learn, because it is beneficial to be able to relax on demand, particularly when dealing with stressful situations, including those times when your tinnitus may be annoying and interfering with your everyday functioning.

There are several different types of relaxation training, including meditation, yoga, and biofeedback. We will describe progressive muscle relaxation (PMR), a procedure originally developed by physiologist Edmund Jacobson in the 1930s, which has since been modified in more recent years. Progressive muscle relaxation has been proven to be a valuable technique in reducing people's tension and subsequent stress levels when practiced on a regular basis, particularly for those individuals who are prone to feeling anxious or uptight. The procedure consists of learning to sequentially tense and then relax the major muscle groups throughout the body.

*The basic components of PMR consist of:*

1. *Learning to tense and then relax various groups of muscles throughout the body. The muscle groups include: left and right hands; arms and biceps; face (forehead, eyes, cheeks, jaw, mouth); neck and throat; shoulders, chest, back and stomach; and upper legs, lower legs and feet.*
2. *Attending to the physical sensations associated with both tension and relaxation. This focus is necessary in order to learn to differentiate between tension and relaxation and to be able to pinpoint tension as it arises in everyday situations.*
3. *After tensing each muscle group for approximately 15 seconds, the tension is slowly released from each muscle group. Attention is then focused on the relaxed muscle group for a minute or even longer. (Henry & Wilson, 2001)*

The reason for asking you to tense the muscles first is to provide a "running start" toward deep relaxation. The tension cycle provides momentum and will give you a good opportunity to become aware of what tension really feels like. It will allow you to compare and appreciate the difference in sensation between tension and relaxation. It is important that you release the tension slowly, not all at once, so you can be aware of the varying degrees of tension.

Learning relaxation is a skill. As with learning any skill (e.g., driving a car, playing a sport, etc.), you will need to practice relaxation on a regular basis in order to achieve maximum skill and benefit. In addition to regular home practice, learning to apply relaxation techniques in everyday situations is important. The primary goal of relaxation training is to be able to relax whenever you need to reduce tension. Situations in which you may need to apply relaxation include those in which you notice that you are under stress, when trying to get to sleep, or when your tinnitus is really loud and annoying.

## *Setting the Scene for Relaxation*

It is important to ensure that the physical setting is appropriate to practice your relaxation in the initial stages. Select a quiet room with dim lighting. Close all windows and doors, and draw the curtains and/or blinds. Seat yourself in a comfortable chair with head and neck support, including armrests. We suggest that you avoid lying down, particularly when first learning progressive muscle relaxation, as many people find they fall asleep. It is obviously not possible to practice this relaxation skill if you are asleep. We also recommend that you remove your glasses, watch, and shoes in order to allow for greater comfort, as well as to reduce any unnecessary external stimulation. To avoid distraction during your practice session, we suggest that you close your eyes. It might also be useful to take the telephone off the hook or turn off your cell phone or pager in order to avoid interruptions to your practice. As you develop your relaxation skills, we suggest that you practice in less comfortable surroundings and try it out even when you are doing normal activities such as cleaning, working, making phone calls, or just going for a walk.

It is important that you avoid tensing any muscles too tightly, as this may produce pain or muscle cramp. This is particularly important if any pain or injury is present (e.g., existing back pain or arthritis). In other words, do not overtense the affected muscle area. With any injury or pain problem, there is likely to be an existing level of tension, so avoid tensing this muscle area and focus on relaxing the muscle.

## *Points to Bear in Mind*

1. *Relaxation Is a Self-Control Technique*
   First, it is important to remember that relaxation is a self-control technique. Research suggests that substantial improvement will occur only when relaxation training is viewed as an active coping skill to be practiced and applied throughout the day. Thus, relaxation involves your active participation in mod-

ifying your responses to stressful events. Stressful situations generally result in tightening the reins of control. Through repeated practice and by learning to release physical tension, you will experience an increased sense of control over your reactions to stress and tension.

2. *Regular Practice Is Required*
   If it is accepted that learning to relax involves learning a skill, like learning a new sport, then it follows that regular practice is essential. We suggest that you practice relaxation training for about 15 to 20 minutes each day for a 4-week period. Thereafter, the skill should be maintained by practicing for 15 to 20 minutes three times per week. However, the applied exercises in everyday situations that we will describe in the following section should be implemented in response to any stressors that you might encounter in your everyday life.

3. *Tune in to "Tension Zones"*
   An important aspect of relaxation involves learning to become more aware of particular "tension zones"—that is, those muscle groups where you are prone to experience tension. Common areas include the neck and shoulders, the stomach, the jaw, and the forehead. We suggest that you do a spot check of your tension areas and concentrate on relaxing these areas throughout the day (e.g., while waiting on a telephone answering system, a supermarket checkout line, in a line of traffic, etc.).

4. *Incorporate Relaxation Training with Other Self-Control Techniques*
   Keep in mind that relaxation training is only one method among many that may be used in controlling tension and stress. Incorporate relaxation into your own personally tailored self-management program that might also include the thought management, attention control, imagery skills, and self-instructional training described in this book.

5. *Falling Asleep*
   During relaxation there is a lowering of tension level and a slowing down of bodily processes. These physical effects are

frequently accompanied by a change in direction of thought processes—there may be a feeling of calmness and a less critical or demanding attitude. In this state there is sometimes a tendency to drift off to sleep. This tendency should be resisted, unless relaxation is being used specifically to overcome a problem of insomnia. The goal of relaxation is to be deeply relaxed while remaining wide awake.

**6.** *Sensations of Losing Control*
High levels of tension may lead to rigid control (bracing oneself in face of stress) and a fear of losing this control when doing relaxation. Some people may experience difficulties or they may be able to relax to a certain stage and be unable to proceed beyond this stage. If you experience such difficulties, we suggest that in the initial stages of practice, the training sessions may be short to begin with, and gradually lengthened as you become more comfortable with relaxing for longer periods. Remember, you are in control—you are gaining control over yourself by letting go of tension.

**7.** *Unusual Physical Sensations*
While the muscles are beginning to unwind, you may experience a number of unusual sensations. These might include feelings of heaviness in parts of your body, floating sensations, tingling sensations, sudden muscle contractions, and so on. Such feelings are common and are no cause for concern. If such feelings are interfering with your practice, we suggest that you open your eyes, breathe more deeply from your diaphragm, and slowly contract your muscles. Then close your eyes and recommence your practice.

**8.** *Concentration Problems*
A commonly reported problem concerns concentration difficulties. It is not possible to concentrate on relaxing for a long period of time. If you experience intruding or competing thoughts, it is important to refocus your attention on relaxation as soon as you are aware that your focus of attention has drifted. One approach that some people find helpful is to just imagine letting the thoughts drift by like fluffy white clouds against a blue sky, observing but not dwelling on them.

# *How to Learn Progressive Muscle Relaxation (PMR)*

*We will instruct you in a PMR procedure using five muscle groups. Listed below are the five muscle groups with suggestions as to how to tense each group.*

1. Left and Right Hands, Arms and Biceps
   *Clench both fists; tighten muscles in lower arms; bring elbows into the back of the chair and press downwards, contracting the biceps muscles (between your elbows and shoulders). Alternatively, stretch your arms out in front of you, clench your fists and tighten the muscles in your arms and hands.*

2. Face
   *Frown at the forehead, squint the eyes, wrinkle the nose, clench your jaw, bite your teeth, pull the side of your mouth outwards, press your tongue hard against the roof of your mouth.*

3. Neck and Throat
   *Press your head firmly against the back of the chair, tightening the muscles in your neck and throat. Alternatively, push your chin down toward your chest but at the same time push upward so as to not allow your chin to touch your chest.*

4. Chest, Shoulders, Back and Stomach
   *Take a deep breath in, hold it; sit forward slightly, push your chest out and bring the shoulder blades together and pull the stomach muscles in, tightly.*

5. Left and Right Upper Leg, Lower Leg and Feet
   *Stretch legs out straight, raise upper legs slightly off the chair, tighten lower legs, and curl toes up toward the ceiling, or down toward the floor. (Henry & Wilson, 2001)*

The five muscle groups described above are progressively tensed and relaxed. Apply tension to each muscle group for approximately 15 seconds (there is no need to be too concerned about the exact timing). After the tension has been slowly released, focus your attention on the relaxed muscle group for about a minute or longer. Repeat this procedure with the remaining muscle groups.

We are aware that many self-help books simply tell people that they should relax, but provide little guidance about the ways in which a professional therapist would assist individuals in that goal. In this book, we provide you with a complete transcript of a relaxation learning session. Obviously, it would be difficult to read the script and to learn to relax simultaneously (although you may indeed be able to achieve this step at a later point in time). The script is provided here so that you can read it through and gain a general understanding of the approach. You may wish to pass the script to a family member or friend who is willing to assist you. Many people enjoy having an assisting role to play and will find it very relaxing even when they are reading it through. The script should be read very slowly and quietly, and in a calm, almost monotonous voice.

In the following section we have also provided a set of basic instructions that can be used to establish a relaxation learning session for yourself to do on your own. However, we suggest that you read the full script first and then move to the abbreviated exercise for self-administration (those instructions follow the full script).

You may also find it useful to make your own audio-cassette tape recording of the relaxation training script provided here. You can do this by recording your own reading (or a friend or family member's reading) of the relaxation script, at a slow, monotonous pace, just like you would read the script when practicing this technique. You can then use this audiotape to assist you with your relaxation practice sessions.

## Self-Assessment Exercise 12: Recording Your Relaxation Practice

Before and after each of your practice sessions, use the monitoring form described in Figure 6.1 to record your ratings of tension at the beginning and at the end of your relaxation training practice. Once again, we suggest that you make photocopies of this form so that you can keep a record of your relaxation practice as well as assess your progress in becoming proficient at this skill.

**FIGURE 6.1** *Self-Assessment Exercise 12: Recording Your Relaxation Practice*

Relaxation is a skill that needs to be learned through regular practice. Practice relaxation at least once a day and record the date and time of your practice on this form. Rate your level of physical tension on a scale of 0 to 10 (0 = extremely relaxed; 10 = extremely tense) both before and after your relaxation practice. You can use this form to monitor your progress in learning to achieve deeper levels of relaxation.

| Date | Time | *Tension* **Before** *Relaxation Practice* *0–10* *0 = extremely relaxed* *10 = extremely tense* | *Tension* **After** *Relaxation Practice* *0–10* *0 = extremely relaxed* *10 = extremely tense* |
|---|---|---|---|
| Example: 8 May | 1:30 P.M. | 8 | 2 |
|  |  |  |  |
|  |  |  |  |
|  |  |  |  |
|  |  |  |  |
|  |  |  |  |
|  |  |  |  |
|  |  |  |  |
|  |  |  |  |
|  |  |  |  |

# *Full Relaxation Script for Home Practice*

*O.K. now just lie / sit back and make yourself as comfortable as possible. Just close your eyes and focus on your breathing. . . . Breathe very gently in and out . . . your breathing is very smooth and rhythmic . . . in and out. Put everything else to one side and just concentrate on your breathing. Focus on the various muscle groups in your body . . . and become aware of the sensations or feelings in the particular muscle groups. . . . With each particular muscle group spend a few minutes focusing your attention on the particular muscle . . . then tense that muscle group and hold the tension for about 15 seconds. . . . Become aware of the tension and tightness . . . following this, slowly release the tension and then focus your attention on the relaxed muscle for about a minute. Sequentially work through this process with each muscle group. The five main muscle groups will be: both your arms and hands; the muscles in your face; the neck and throat; the shoulders, chest, back, and stomach; and finally, both legs and feet. Remember that the aim of the exercises will be to become as physically comfortable and relaxed as possible.*

*Now, re-focus your attention on your breathing . . . smoothly in and out . . . in and out . . . and just think to yourself the word "relax" each time you breathe out . . . just keep thinking the word "relax" each time you breathe out.*

*Now, focus your attention on the muscles in your hands and arms . . . both your hands and arms. Just spend a few moments getting your attention on to that group of muscles. Try to become aware of the physical sensations which you feel in your hands and arms. . . . Try to be aware of whether they feel warm or cold . . . whether they feel heavy or light . . . even try to be aware of the sensations in each of your fingers . . . one by one . . . even the very tips of your fingers. . . . Now, stop thinking the word "relax." . . . In a moment think to yourself the word "tense" and when you do, tense the muscles in both your hands and both your arms . . . make the muscles feel firm and tight. O.K. now, think the word "tense." . . . Add the tension to your hands and arms to the point that it feels noticeably tense. . . . Notice how tight the muscles in your hands and arms feel. . . . Hold the tension for a moment . . . and now "relax" . . . just slowly let the tension go. Bit by bit . . . let a little tension go each time you breathe out. . . . As you breathe out begin again to think the word "relax." . . . Keep letting the tension go . . . step by step . . . feel the tension falling away . . . draining away. . . . Your hands and arms are feeling more and more relaxed . . . relax them completely . . . concentrating on what it feels like to let the tension go. . . . Just let the muscles go loose and floppy . . . loose and floppy, just like a rag doll . . . and just imagine that if you tried to lift up one of your arms and hands it would feel loose and relaxed. . . . Your arms and hands feel pleasantly relaxed and comfortable. . . . There is no need for any tension and tightness . . . just relax . . . and your breathing is still smooth and rhythmic . . . in and out . . . gently in and out . . . just relax. . . .*

*Now move on to the next muscle group. . . . Focus on the sensations in the muscles in your face. . . . Focus all of your attention on your facial muscles . . . the muscles in your forehead . . . around your eyes . . . your cheeks . . . nose . . . mouth and jaw. . . . Become aware of the sensations in those muscles . . . just keep breathing smoothly and rhythmically in and out and keep thinking the word "relax" with each breath out. . . . Keep focusing on the muscles in your face. . . . Become aware of the sensations. . . . Now, stop thinking the word "relax" . . . and in a moment think to yourself the word "tense" and tense all of the muscles in your face. . . . Frown at the forehead, squint up the muscles around your eyes, tighten the muscles in your cheeks, around your mouth, tongue and jaw . . . make the muscles feel firm and tight.*

*O.K. now, think the word "tense." . . . Add the tension to all of the muscles in your face to the point that it feels noticeably tense. . . . Notice how tight the muscles in your face feel. . . . Hold the tension for a moment . . . and now think the word "relax" . . . just slowly let the tension go . . . bit by bit . . . let a little tension go each time you breathe out . . . as you breathe out begin again to think the word "relax." . . . Keep letting the tension go . . . step by step . . . feel the tension falling away . . . draining away. . . . Just smooth out the muscles in your face . . . relax the muscles in your forehead, around your eyes, cheeks, mouth, jaw. . . . Your facial muscles are feeling more and more relaxed . . . relax them completely . . . concentrate on what it feels like to let the tension go . . . just let the muscles go loose and relaxed . . . loose and relaxed. . . . All of the muscles in your face feel pleasantly relaxed and comfortable . . . there is no need for any tension and tightness . . . just relax . . . and your breathing is still smooth and rhythmic . . . in and out . . . gently in and out . . . just keep thinking the word "relax" with each breath out.*

*And now move on to the next muscle group. . . . Focus on the sensations in the muscles in your neck and throat. . . . Focus all of your attention on your neck and throat. . . . Become aware of the sensations in those muscles. . . . Just keep breathing smoothly and rhythmically in and out and keep thinking the word "relax" with each breath out. . . . Keep focusing on the muscles in your neck and throat . . . become aware of the sensations. . . . Now, stop thinking the word "relax." . . . Think to yourself the word "tense" and tense all of the muscles in your neck and throat by pulling your chin down toward your chest but at the same time setting up a resistance and not allowing your chin and chest to touch. . . . Add the tension to all of the muscles in your neck and throat to the point that it feels noticeably tense. . . . Notice how tight the muscles in your neck and throat feel. . . . Hold the tension for a moment . . . and now think the word "relax" . . . just slowly let the tension go . . . bit by bit . . . let a little tension go each time you breathe out. . . . As you breathe out begin again to think the word "relax" . . . keep letting the tension go . . . step by step . . . feel the tension falling away . . . draining away. . . . Just smooth out the muscles in your neck and throat . . . relax the muscles in your neck and throat. . . . The muscles are feeling more and more relaxed . . . relax them completely. . . . Concentrate on what it feels like to let the tension go . . . just let the muscles go loose and relaxed . . . loose and relaxed. . . . All of the muscles in your neck and throat feel pleasantly relaxed and comfortable. . . . There is no need for any tension and tightness . . . just relax . . . and your breathing is still smooth and rhythmic . . . in and out . . . gently in and out . . . just keep thinking the word "relax" with each breath out.*

*And now move on to the next muscle group. . . . Focus on the sensations in the muscles in your shoulders, chest, back, and stomach. . . . Focus all of your attention on these muscles . . . become aware of the sensations in those muscles. . . . Just keep breathing smoothly and rhythmically in and out and keep thinking the word "relax" with each breath out. . . . Keep focusing on the muscles in your shoulders, chest, back and stomach . . . become aware of the sensations. . . . Now, stop thinking the word "relax." . . . Now, in a moment think to yourself the word "tense" and as you do so, tense all of the muscles in your shoulders, chest, back, and stomach. You can do this by taking a deep breath in . . . holding it . . . pulling your shoulder blades back . . . and tightening your stomach muscles.*

*O.K. now, "tense"... breathe in... hold it... add the tension to all of the muscles in your shoulders, chest, back, and stomach.... Feel the tension... notice how tight the muscles feel... hold the tension for a moment... and now "relax"... just slowly let the tension go... bit by bit... let a little tension go each time you breathe out.... As you breathe out begin again to think the word "relax."... Keep letting the tension go... step by step... feel the tension falling away... draining away... just smooth out the muscles in your shoulders... just let them drop.... lower your shoulder blades.... Relax the muscles in your chest, back, and stomach.... The muscles are feeling more and more relaxed... relax them completely... concentrate on what it feels like to let the tension go... just let the muscles go loose and relaxed... loose and relaxed.... All of the muscles feel pleasantly relaxed and comfortable.... There is no need for any tension and tightness... just relax... and your breathing is still smooth and rhythmic... in and out... gently in and out.... Make sure you are breathing from your diaphragm... pushing your stomach out with each breath in... and just keep thinking the word "relax" with each breath out.*

*And now move on to the next muscle group.... Begin to focus on the sensations in the muscles in both your legs and both your feet.... Focus all of your attention on these muscles... the muscles in your upper legs, knees, lower legs and both your feet... become aware of the sensations in those muscles.... Just keep breathing smoothly and rhythmically in and out and keep thinking the word "relax" with each breath out.... Keep focusing on the muscles in both your legs and feet... even focus on the sensations in the tips of your toes... become aware of the sensations.... Now, stop thinking the word "relax."... In a moment, for the last time, think to yourself the word "tense" and tense the muscles in both your legs and your feet. You can do this by stretching your legs out and pointing your toes up toward the ceiling or down towards the floor... tightening all of the muscles from your upper legs down through to your toes.*

*O.K. now, think to yourself the word "tense."... Add the tension to all of the muscles in your legs and feet to the point that they feel noticeably tense.... Notice how tight the muscles in your legs and feet feel... hold the tension for a moment... and now "relax."... Just slowly let the tension go... bit by bit... let a little tension go each time you breathe out.... As you breathe out begin again to think the word "relax"... keep letting the tension go... step by step... feel the tension falling away...draining away...just relax the muscles in your legs and your feet.... Your legs and feet are feeling more and more relaxed...relax them completely...concentrate on what it feels like to let the tension go.... Just let the muscles go loose and relaxed...loose and relaxed.... All of the muscles in your legs and feet feel pleasantly relaxed and comfortable...there is no need for any tension and tightness...just relax...and your breathing is still smooth and rhythmic...in and out...gently in and out...just keep thinking the word "relax" with each breath out.*

*Your whole body feels pleasantly relaxed and comfortable.... There is no need for any tension or tightness.... Just check the various muscle groups to see if any tension has crept back in...and if you notice any signs of tension just concentrate on letting it go.*

*Check your hands and arms...make sure they are relaxed.... Check the muscles in your face...your forehead, around your eyes, cheeks, mouth and jaw.*

*Check the muscles in your neck and throat...check the muscles in your shoulders, chest, back and stomach...and finally check the muscles in both your legs and your feet.... Your whole body feels pleasantly relaxed and comfortable...at peace and at ease.... Your breathing is smooth and rhythmic...gently in...and out.... And now just spend a few quiet moments enjoying the sensations of feeling relaxed.... Your breathing is still smooth and rhythmic in and out.*

*O.K. now in a moment begin to count backwards from 5 through to 1.... As you count begin to slowly open your eyes and on the count of 1 your eyes will be wide open, you will remain feeling pleasantly relaxed and comfortable but you will also feel quite alert and ready to continue on with the day. (Henry & Wilson, 2001)*

## *Abbreviated Script for Self-Guided Relaxation Practice*

Listed below is a set of instructions that you can follow in order to learn to do relaxation on your own. We describe the key steps in relaxation as they might be applied to the first muscle group (i.e., both hands and arms). Once you have mastered this muscle group, simply repeat the process to learn how to relax the remaining four muscle groups (i.e., face; neck and throat; chest, shoulders, back, and stomach; and both legs and feet).

1. Read through the following brief script:
   - Spend a few moments focusing your attention on your breathing.
   - Think the word *relax* each time you breathe out.
   - Focus your attention on the muscles in your hands and arms.
   - Spend a few moments becoming aware of the physical sensations in these muscles.
   - Now, think the word *tense* and tense the muscles in both your hands and arms.
   - Hold the tension for about 15 seconds.
   - Now, think the word *relax* as you breathe out, and slowly release the tension from your hands and arms.
   - Once you have slowly released the tension, focus your attention on the relaxed muscles in your hands and arms for about one minute.
2. Read through the script one more time.
3. Now try the exercise with your eyes closed.
4. Read through the script again to see if you missed any of the steps.
5. Now try the exercise again with your eyes closed.
6. Proceed to use the same script (points 1 to 5) for the remaining four major muscle groups (i.e., face; neck and throat; chest, shoulders, back, and stomach; and both legs and feet).
7. Reread the script at the beginning of your next practice session.
8. When you have become familiar with the script you can omit the reading part of this exercise.

## Modified Relaxation Training Procedures

### PMR Using Four Muscle Groups

The five-muscle PMR technique can be modified in a number of ways in order to strengthen your skill in achieving deeper and more rapid levels of relaxation. One modification is to collapse the five muscle groups down to four. The muscle groups then might consist of: (1) both hands and arms; (2) face, neck, and throat; (3) shoulders, chest, back, and stomach; and (4) both legs and feet. At this point you might begin to move through the muscle groups at a faster rate. Other modifications include practicing relaxation training via recall, relaxation via counting, and conditioned relaxation. A description of each of these techniques is provided next.

## Relaxation via Recall

Relaxation via recall differs from previous procedures in that it does *not* require you to tense your muscles. It does require full use of your increased ability to *focus* on tension and relaxation. Relaxation via recall employs the four muscle groups just described and involves two sequential processes:

1. Careful focusing of your attention on any tension in a particular muscle group
2. Recalling the feelings you have learned to associate with release of that tension when practicing the original PMR exercise, and then spending 30 to 45 seconds relaxing any tension detected

Essentially, the procedure for relaxation via recall is the same as the tension-release technique (used in the traditional PMR exercise); the only difference between these two procedures is that the tension cycle is eliminated with this technique. You can use the following script to guide your practice of the relaxation via recall procedure. Read through the script several times to familiarize yourself with the procedure as it might be applied to the first muscle group (i.e., both hands and arms). Then seat yourself in a quiet environment, make yourself comfortable, and close your eyes. Practice relaxation via recall for the four muscle groups.

*Focus all of your attention on the muscles in both your arms and hands and very carefully identify any feelings of tightness or tension that might be present there now. Notice where the tension is and what it feels like. After a few moments, think to yourself the word "relax,"...just recall what it was like when you released the tension in the muscles in both your hands and arms,...just letting them go and allowing them to become more and more deeply relaxed. Spend about 30–45 seconds on this relaxation phase, before moving onto the next muscle group, and repeat the process for the remaining 3 muscle groups. (Henry & Wilson, 2001)*

## Relaxation via Counting

A further extension of the relaxation via recall technique involves a procedure designed to allow relaxation to become even deeper. The procedure aims to provide further focus of attention on each of your major muscle groups, and to allow relaxation to become even more comfortable. In the first stage, you simply repeat the relaxation via recall technique. Following this, you can introduce a counting technique to focus your attention further on the sensations of relaxation. That is, as you remain very deeply and comfortably relaxed, slowly begin to count mentally from 1 to 10. As you count, allow all the muscles throughout your body to become even more deeply and comfortably relaxed on each count. Just focus your attention on all the muscles in your body and notice them as they become even more and more deeply relaxed as you count from 1 to 10. This relaxation via counting technique is most effective when the counting is paced to coincide with your breaths out.

A further refinement of the relaxation via recall procedure is to use a technique that consists solely of mentally counting from 1 to 10 and giving self-instructions to induce a deep and comfortable state of relaxation. This technique is useful as a time-saving device in everyday settings—for example, in real-life stress situations, such as at work or in traffic. Use the following script to guide your practice of this technique. Once again, read through the script to familiarize yourself with the procedure, then practice this with your eyes closed.

*Just focus on your breathing, gently in and out and think to yourself the word "relax" on each breath out. Focus on the muscles in your body.*

*Become aware of any tension or tightness. Begin to mentally count to yourself from 1 to 10, and, as you count, allow all the muscles throughout your body to become deeply and comfortably relaxed on each count. Just focus your attention on all the muscles in your body and notice them as they become more and more deeply relaxed as you count from 1 to 10. O.K., 1, 2, notice your arms and hands becoming more and more relaxed now; . . . 3, 4, focusing on the muscles of the face, neck, and throat as they now become deeply relaxed; . . . 5, 6, allow the muscles in your chest, shoulders, back, and stomach to become more and more relaxed; . . . 7, 8, notice the muscles in your legs and feet becoming deeply relaxed, more completely relaxed; . . . 9 and 10, your whole body is more deeply and comfortably relaxed, just completely relax. (Henry & Wilson, 2001)*

## Conditioned Relaxation

One further modification to PMR is known as conditioned relaxation. The goal of this technique is to enable you to achieve relaxation in response to a self-produced cue (e.g., saying the word *relax*). To use this technique we recommend that you use PMR or relaxation via recall to become deeply relaxed. Once relaxed, focus all your attention on your breathing and then subvocalize a cue word (i.e., say a "relaxing" word of your choice) on each breath out. Some examples of cue words that you might think to yourself include *calm, control,* and *relax.* Continue this process, repeating the cue word in synchrony with each breath out for 15 to 20 pairings (e.g., "calm 1," "calm 2," . . . "calm 20"). We suggest that you practice this procedure at the end of your daily formal PMR practice. With regular practice, an association is built up between the subvocalized word and the relaxed state, whereby the word alone becomes capable of creating a state of relaxation. The subvocalized word has therefore become a "cue" for relaxation. Once you have learned the association between the deeply relaxed state and a self-produced cue word, and have learned to use such cues to produce relaxation, you can apply this technique to reduce tension in everyday situations. You may find that you can use an image of a favorite place or a piece of music in a similar fashion.

## Slow Breathing Exercise

Slow (diaphragmatic) breathing is another portable and effective means of achieving a calm and relaxed state. This exercise involves regular practice. To begin, place your hands on your abdomen (stomach). Take a deep breath in and notice that as you breathe in your abdomen moves out toward your hands. As you breathe in think to yourself the words "in, 2, 3." Then breathe out while thinking to yourself "relax, 2, 3" and notice that your abdomen lowers. Repeat this process 10 times.

## *Conclusion*

In this chapter we described several methods of relaxation. We suggest that you schedule regular daily practice of the formal four muscle group PMR procedure, which consists of the tension-release phase. As you begin to make progress in developing skill in relaxation we recommend that you gradually move from relaxing in quiet, comfortable places to increasingly more difficult locations. For example, from a reclining position, you might move relaxation practice to an upright chair in the living room, or while typing in a study, eating in a cafeteria, standing in your bedroom, waiting in a ticket line or for a train, and walking outside. You should also begin to employ the relaxation via recall, counting or conditioned methods as mini-practice throughout the day. Given that these abbreviated procedures do not involve the tension cycle, they are more portable relaxation techniques that can be easily applied in everyday situations. Try to engage in mini-relaxation practice in a variety of situations, such as when you are waiting for a bus, stopped at a traffic light, standing in a line, and so on.

Another way of ensuring that you are applying relaxation in everyday situations is to become more aware of your particular "tension areas"—those muscle groups in which you are prone to experience tension. Common areas include the neck and shoulders, the stomach, the jaw, and the forehead. During the day do a "spot check" of your tension areas and deliberately relax them as soon as you notice any increase in tension.

We recommend that you begin to use the relaxation training techniques to deal with the tinnitus when it is especially bothersome or when you are experiencing difficulty with sleeping. Try to identify situations in which you would like to become more relaxed. Maximum benefit is likely to be obtained when you use relaxation techniques to deal both with the stress associated with tinnitus and with other more general everyday stress, such as family or work problems.

# 7

## *Attention Control Techniques*

*One really big problem that I have with tinnitus is that it just seems to consume me! It is everywhere I go. When I have a bad day I just can't seem to focus on anything else. I can't get my mind off the noise. It becomes my whole world! Nothing makes a difference. I find I worry about it more and it gets louder and louder. The louder it gets, the more impossible it becomes trying to ignore it. My family tells me to just forget about it. What do they know, none of them has tinnitus. They tell me to just read the paper or something. They think it is so simple. But once the tinnitus has caught my attention, I cannot concentrate on anything else—no way!*

In Chapters 4 and 5 we described methods by which you can learn to change the way you think about your tinnitus. By learning to think about the tinnitus in a more constructive and helpful way, you can alter your emotional response. This approach may be helpful in reducing feelings of depression, anxiety, anger, and other troublesome emotions. The ability to identify problematic thoughts, to challenge your thinking, and to develop more constructive and helpful thoughts are very important skills in adapting to tinnitus or any other difficulty. Sometimes the tinnitus may be very intrusive, occupying your attention far more than you would like. Perhaps these times are those when you perceive the tinnitus to be particularly loud or when you are trying to fall asleep. In such situations you may wish that you could control the focus of your attention.

In this chapter we will instruct you in some methods that can help you achieve this goal. These methods include attention control, imagery training, and distraction techniques. These self-control strategies can be combined with the relaxation techniques that we described in the previous chapter. The main aim of these techniques is to assist you in learning how to switch the focus of your attention from one thing to another, and to teach you that this process can be brought under voluntary control.

One common complaint about tinnitus is the extent to which it seizes a person's attention, making it difficult to focus on anything else. This can lead to heightened distress and a feeling of helplessness. The techniques described in this chapter are designed to help you develop skills in refocusing your attention from your tinnitus to other internal or external sensations. These techniques can give you a greater sense of self-control over the tinnitus at times when it might be particularly troublesome as well as provide a further means of reducing tinnitus-related distress.

## *The Nature of Human Attention*

The process of attention has several qualities that are significant for understanding its use in the management of tinnitus. At any given time, numerous stimuli may compete for a person's attention. These stimuli may either be internal or external. Examples of *internal stimuli* include thoughts, mental images, and bodily sensations (e.g., body temperature, thirst, hunger, need to go to the bathroom), pain, and tinnitus). *External stimuli* may include outside noises, light, temperature, pollution, odors, and visual objects. The primary focus of attention at any one point in time depends on a number of factors, such as how important or relevant it is to the individual at that moment. The mind will naturally focus on certain stimuli and selectively ignore others. People may simply notice one stimulus, but quickly switch their focus of attention to another one, for example. It may be difficult to cease paying attention to unpleasant sensations (e.g., extreme temperature, physical pain, thirst) unless a person deliberately shifts the focus of attention to other objects, feelings, or sensations. However, people do have some control over this process, and can exert a surprising degree of influence over the direction of their attention.

## *Attention Control and Tinnitus*

The main aim of attention control techniques is to learn to switch attention from one stimulus (e.g., object, sensation, thought, activity) to another at will. Through the use of attention control techniques you can develop skill in refocusing your attention from your tinnitus onto other stimuli, internal or external. Sensations can be brought into the foreground of your awareness, or be allowed to remain in the background. These techniques can help provide you with a heightened sense of control over your tinnitus, especially on occasions when it is a source of annoyance. It is important to recognize that the idea is not so much to stop thinking about the tinnitus, but to learn to direct your attention both to and from the tinnitus under your own control. With regular practice you will become increasingly confident that you can exert control over the focus of your attention.

In the next section we describe a series of attention control exercises. Exercise 1 is designed to illustrate the general principle of attention control. In Exercise 2 we extend this basic procedure, and in Exercise 3 we address tinnitus more directly. Read through each exercise several times and then try practicing the procedures with your eyes closed. This will reduce any potential visual distractions and help you remain more focused on the tasks.

## *Training in Attention Control*

### Exercise 1: Internal-Physical Sensations

Seat yourself in a comfortable chair, close your eyes, and focus your attention on your breathing. Breathe very slowly and rhythmically in, then out—very gently in, and out. Become aware of your breathing process—the *in* phase and the *out* phase, in and out. Try to focus your attention on this process and become aware of the very point in time when the process reverses—where your breathing changes direction from *in* to *out*. Imagine this is somewhat like the waves on a beach, rolling in and receding out. Just keep focusing your attention on your breathing, in and out.

As your attention focuses on your breathing, you probably haven't been aware of the sensations in your hands, even the tips of your fingers. Just gently shift your attention and your awareness to your hands. Try to mentally identify each finger without moving it; become aware of each of your fingers, quietly focusing your attention on them.

Since you have been focusing all your attention on your fingers, you have probably not been aware of your breathing; it probably receded into the background. Now just calmly refocus your attention back to your breathing—your breathing gently proceeds from *in* to *out,* to *in* to *out,* and so on. Quietly focus on such a soothing process as your breathing changes from *in* to *out*.

And now, as your attention focuses more closely on your breathing, you probably have not been aware of the sensations in your toes and feet. Shift your attention to the extreme end of your body. Become aware of the sensations in your toes. Visualize each separate toe and concentrate your attention on each one as you picture it.

And once again, now as you focus on your toes and feet, your breathing has probably receded into the background. Refocus your attention to your breathing—in and out, in and out.

Try to think of your awareness and attention as a searchlight—you can direct it onto whatever you choose to focus on. Just see how the searchlight can be directed onto whatever you choose. Focus it on your breathing, to your hands, to your breathing, to your feet and toes—you can control the focus of your attention and awareness. You can redirect your attention throughout your body—from your breathing, to your hands, and then to your feet and toes. Now spend a few quiet moments focusing on your breathing and allowing your muscles to relax. Breathe gently in and out, in and out. After a few quiet moments, open your eyes.

- When you were paying attention to some specific part of your body, such as your hands, did you notice that other parts of your body merge into the background, or that you are not aware of them? By using attention control techniques, sensations can be focused on and brought into the foreground, or they can be ignored and allowed to remain in the background. Now try the second exercise, which is an extension of the basic procedure.

## Exercise 2: Internal versus External Sensations

Make yourself comfortable and close your eyes. Spend a few moments focusing on your breathing—just breathe gently *in* and *out, in* and *out, in* and *out.* Now practice switching your attention. Learn to control it and direct it, just like a searchlight. You can control the focus of your awareness and attention—divert it and focus on one thing, then shift it to another. Ask yourself the question: Where is my attention now? Is it focused on internal sensations inside your body, or on external sensations arising from inside the room, or perhaps on sensations outside the room?

Now, focus your attention on physical sensations. Be aware of the air temperature on your skin. Is it warm or cool? Notice the sensations on your arms and hands. Now try to become aware of other sensations, movements, or sounds within your body. Also notice that whatever thoughts or images come into your mind, these interfere with your awareness and attention.

Now, refocus your attention. Focus on the sounds and sensations within the room. What can you hear? What noises are there in the room? Mentally identify the noises. Now refocus by switching your attention to the sounds and sensations outside of this room—maybe in the hallway, or the next room, or outside in the open. What can you hear outside? Do you notice voices, laughter, birds chirping, the wind, traffic, machinery, footsteps, aircraft? Try to identify any outside noises.

Now refocus your attention. Concentrate on the sensations in your feet. Next, focus just on your toes. Picture each one.

And now, focus your attention back onto your breathing. Breathe gently *in* and *out, in* and *out*. Spend a few quiet moments focusing on your breathing and allow all the muscles in your body to relax. After a few moments, slowly open your eyes.

- Did you notice the ways you can shift the focus of your attention—from internal physical sensations, to your immediate external environment, and to the further external environment?

You have control of the focus of your attention. With regular practice you can increase your skill in attention control and learn to be confident about your ability to deliberately refocus your attention from one thing to another. Now practice exercise 3, in which tinnitus will be directly addressed.

## Exercise 3: Physical versus Sound Sensations

Make yourself comfortable and close your eyes. Once again, begin by focusing your attention on your breathing, gently *in* and *out, in* and *out*.

Now focus your awareness on the noises in your head—tune into the noises. What can you hear? Spend a few moments listening to the noises. Now refocus your attention to your hands. Slowly identify each of your fingers. Now redirect your attention. Shift it further down your body, focusing on your feet. Be aware of your right foot and your left foot, then slowly become aware of each toe. Next, redirect your attention and focus on your breathing, *in* and *out*. Notice the point where your breathing changes from *in* to *out*, to *in* to *out*. Spend a few moments becoming aware of your breathing.

Now, what external sounds can you hear? Spend a few moments becoming aware of any external sounds and try to identify the source of those sounds.

Focus back onto the noises in your head, paying attention to the various noises. Now quickly redirect your attention. Focus on external noises in the room and outside. What can you hear? Spend a few moments trying to identify any external sounds. Next, focus again on physical sensations—notice the air temperature, the sensations on the skin of your hands, the palms of your hands.

Now allow yourself to spend a minute shifting your attention from internal to external sensations; deliberately refocus your attention. Notice that you can only focus on one thing at a time. Practice moving deliberately back and forth between the noises in your head, physical sensations, and external sensations. After about five minutes, focus your attention back to your breathing. Spend a few quiet moments focusing on your breathing and at the same time allowing all your muscles to relax. After a few moments, slowly open your eyes.

## Summary of Attention Control Techniques

There are three important points to keep in mind when practicing attention control exercises:

1. The focus of your attention is, to a large extent, under voluntary control (provided that you are aware of the current focus).
2. You can learn to control the focus of your attention under various conditions.
3. By exerting control over your attention, tinnitus-related distress will be reduced at certain times.

Daily practice is essential to develop your skill in attention control. We recommend that you practice the exercises for 10 to 20 minutes each day.

Of course, we recognize that for many people, tinnitus appears to have some edge over other stimuli in its ability to command attention. Numerous individuals report that when their tinnitus is particularly troublesome, they find it difficult to attend to anything else. This is another similarity that tinnitus shares with chronic pain. Many of the techniques we describe in this chapter have been adapted from similar approaches that have been found to be highly effective in managing pain. Like pain, tinnitus may represent a challenge to overcome, but we suggest that it is well worth attempting to see just how much control can be achieved.

It might be useful to ask yourself whether you have noticed that, when your attention has been focused on something else, the tinnitus is sometimes less noticeable. Most people can think of examples of this phenomenon. Some examples might include working on your computer, repairing your car, playing golf, watching a favorite television program, sailing, watching football, listening to a friend tell you some gossip, and so on. From our clinical experience with people who have tinnitus, these methods can prove to be as effective as when they are applied to chronic pain patients.

Finally, we would like to emphasize that the idea is not so much to stop thinking about, or focusing on, the tinnitus. Rather, *the aim of attention control is for you to learn to develop the skill of being able to direct attention both to and from the tinnitus*. This point is very important, as the main goal is to build up the attention control skill per se, and for you to develop your confidence in being able to control the focus of your attention. With regular practice you can learn to redirect your attention from one source of stimuli to another. This point is crucial, since it is difficult, if not impossible, to stop paying attention to unpleasant sensations (e.g., tinnitus or pain) unless one refocuses his or her attention on to other more pleasant or even neutral things. In the next section we will describe some other attentional control methods that involve the use of mental imagery.

## *Imagery Training*

Imagery techniques, which share some similarities to the attention control exercises just described, can also be used as a self-control method for coping with tinnitus-related distress. The main aim of using these techniques is to develop the ability to focus attention on sensory experiences in the mind by creating novel mental images, or by recalling places and events from past experiences. As with the attention control exercises, by deliberately focusing on mental images, other sensations will merge into the background. Essentially, imagery techniques provide you with a means of focusing on something pleasant, or even neutral, rather than focusing on whatever might be unpleasant in any given situation. Thus, imagery represents another method of attention control that can be used in a wide range of situations. These occasions might include times when you are particularly aware of your tinnitus (e.g., trying to fall asleep or dealing with noisy or quiet environments), or when dealing with a variety of stressful everyday events (e.g., waiting in a line, being stuck in a traffic jam, waiting for a dental appointment, or receiving an injection).

Typically, when people use imagery, they tend to focus on the visual modality (i.e., what they can see in their "mind's eye"). Mental images can be strengthened by using all (or most) sensory modalities. That is, when you use imagery, it is helpful not only to visualize the image but also to focus on the following:

1. What you can hear (e.g., chirping birds, people in conversation, waves crashing, wind, crackling fire, music)
2. What you can smell (e.g., salt air, burning embers on a log-fire, flowers, fish and chips, perfume)
3. What you can feel and touch (e.g., warmth of sun, cool wind or breeze, cool water)
4. What you can taste (e.g., refreshing iced tea drink, chocolate cake, clam chowder)

By focusing on all of the sensory modalities, you may enrich your use of imagery, creating a more absorbing and enjoyable experience.

There are individual differences in the extent to which people can use mental imagery. Some people find that imagery techniques are easy to use, as they are able to visualize images quite clearly; others experience more difficulty. However, regular practice may help to strengthen a person's ability to use such techniques. Before describing some imagery exercises for you to practice, there are three points that we wish to emphasize:

1. By developing this skill, tinnitus-related distress can be reduced at certain times (e.g., when the tinnitus is especially

loud, when you are trying to fall asleep, when you are in quiet or noisy places, when your attentional focus is drawn to your tinnitus).

2. Many people can learn to develop mental images under voluntary control.
3. With practice, you can learn to engage in mental imagery.

## Exercise 1: Introduction to Imagery Training

In this first exercise, we simply try to extend the range and richness of your imagery ability by taking you through each sense (sight, touch, hearing, smell and taste), one at a time.

### *Exercise 1.1: Sense of Sight*

First, collect together the following objects:

- Pen
- Cup
- Glass
- Comb

Place these objects on a table in front of you. Read through the following exercise and then begin your practice session:

- Spend a few moments looking at the *pen* on the table in front of you.
- Examine the pen closely, looking at its color, shape, texture, and form.
- Spend a few moments looking at the pen.
- Now close your eyes and imagine the pen in your mind. Focus on this until you can see a clear image in your mind.
- Open your eyes and look at the pen. Examine it again for a few moments.
- Now close your eyes and once again capture the image of the pen in your mind.
- Next, spend a few moments looking at the *cup* on the table in front of you.

- Examine the cup closely, looking at its color, shape, texture, and form.
- Spend a few moments looking at the cup.
- Now close your eyes and imagine the cup in your mind. Focus on this until you can see a clear image in your mind.
- Open your eyes and look at the cup. Examine it again for a few moments.
- Now close your eyes and once again capture the image of the cup in your mind.
- Repeat this exercise to practice visualizing the *glass* and then the *comb*.
- Once you are able to visualize these four everyday objects, you can extend the exercise by trying to mentally change the colors of the objects. For example, if the pen is blue, try to imagine a black pen or a green pen; if the comb is black, imagine it is pink.

### *Exercise 1.2: Sense of Touch*

Now let's try experimenting with different textures. Imagine each of the following objects:

- Apple (smooth, hard, cool)
- Satin cloth (very smooth, soft)
- Ice cube (very smooth, cold)
- Piece of fresh bread (very soft, room temperature)
- Piece of toast (rough, warm)
- Mug of coffee/tea (smooth, hard, very warm)
- Wet soap (wet, soft, slippery)

Although you will probably focus on their visual appearance, we want you to allow most of your attention to fall on the sensations that you can experience if you were to imagine that you were actually touching these objects. Should you find this difficult, you could begin by repeating the previous exercise. Most of the objects in the preceding list are probably located somewhere in your home. For example, get an apple from the kitchen. With your eyes open, hold it in your hands and become aware of how it feels to touch it. Then put the apple down, close your eyes and try to capture the sensation of holding an apple in your imagination. Now try imagining each of the other objects listed.

The following scenes also involve sensation of touch, but they apply to more general bodily sensations. Try to imagine:

- Standing barefoot on pebbles
- Standing barefoot on warm sand
- Standing barefoot on grass
- Placing your hand into warm water
- Placing your hand into cold water
- Feeling the sun on your back
- Feeling a hat on your head

### Exercise 1.3: Sense of Hearing

Now try to imagine the following sounds:

- Waterfall
- Fountain
- Ocean waves
- Running tap water
- Airplane
- Siren
- Water over rocks in a stream or in rapids
- Electric fan
- Static on radio
- Car horn
- Birds
- Whistling kettle
- Insects in trees
- Stomach rumbling

### Exercise 1.4: Sense of Smell

Now try to imagine the following smells:

- Coffee
- Garlic

- Beer
- Cut grass
- Old book
- Perfume
- Disinfectant
- Fries
- Chocolate
- Cow manure
- Bacon

### *Exercise 1.5: Sense of Taste*

Now try to imagine the following tastes:

- Toothpaste
- Onion
- Orange juice
- Fried egg
- Chocolate chip cookies
- Muffin
- Licorice
- Corn chips
- Avocado
- Sour cream
- Parmesan cheese
- Cheddar cheese
- Blue cheese
- Chili
- Cabanossi or salami

# *Imagery Training Combining the Senses*

Let's now look at how you might use imagery techniques that begin to combine the various sensory modalities. In the next exercise we will combine a number of senses: sight, touch, smell, and taste. To complete the exercise you will need a lemon.

## Exercise 2: Lemons and Oranges

Place a lemon on the table and read the following text (adapted from Bakal, 1982):

> Imagine a fresh, ripe lemon. You can clearly see the shiny yellow of its skin. See the texture, the bumps on the skin. You are holding the lemon with one hand, and in the other hand you are holding a knife. Cut the lemon in half. As you slice the lemon you can see and feel the juice running onto your fingers and hands. Smell the strong citrus lemon juice. Now taste the lemon, the sharp lemon juice—your mouth puckers up—taste the lemon.... And now, let the image fade away.... It fades away completely. And slowly open your eyes.

Now close your eyes while holding the lemon, and imagine the scene that you have just read. You may wish to read it again in order to remember what you need to do (in your imagination) with the lemon. Read the text again now.

Next, imagine the same scene with an orange (or some other fruit that is not actually present). Imagine the bright orange color, feel the juice of the orange running down your hand, smell it, and taste it. Now you might like to eat the orange!

## Exercise 3: Combining the Senses Using Singular Objects

Listed here are some objects that allow for a combination of various senses to be explored. Try to imagine each object. Once again, many of these will probably be located somewhere in your home. Should you have any difficulty imagining any of the objects, try to locate the object and practice the exercise with the object present. For example, if you find it difficult to imagine the sight, touch, taste, and smell of toothpaste, then get your tube of toothpaste and explore how it looks, smells, tastes, and feels. Then close your eyes and practice imagining all of this in your mind.

### Exercise 3.1: Sight and Hearing

Imagine the following:

- A bird chirping—What can you see? What can you hear? What kind of bird is it?
- Leaves rustling in the wind—What can you see? What can you hear?
- Fireworks—What colors or patterns can you see? What can you hear?

### Exercise 3.2: Sight, Touch, and Hearing

Imagine the following objects: What can you see? What can you feel? What can you hear?

- Watch or clock
- Small bag of coins
- Two die
- Electric fan

### Exercise 3.3: Sight, Touch, and Smell

- Imagine a cake of perfumed soap—What can you see? What can you feel? What can you smell?

### Exercise 3.4: Sight, Hearing, and Smell

- Imagine a wood fire—What can you see? What can you hear? What sensations can you feel? What can you smell?

### Exercise 3.5: Sight, Hearing, Taste, and Smell

Imagine the following and try to capture what you can see, hear, taste, and smell:

- Coke in a glass
- Coffee percolating
- Champagne

*Exercise 3.6: Sight, Hearing, Taste, Smell,*
*and Touch*

Imagine the following and try to identify what you can see, hear, taste, smell, and touch:

- Roasting chestnuts
- Blowing bubbles through a straw in a can of your favorite soda
- Munching into a hamburger (with everything!)

# Imagery Training for More Complex Scenes

Now we are going to progress to more complex images such as being in a particular place, perhaps a favorite location or some place where you have spent an enjoyable holiday. The idea is to learn to move from visualizing single objects to gradually being able to build-up a series of mental images into a detailed scene.

## Exercise 4: Combining the Senses Using Personal Photographs

Go through your personal photo collection and select two photos of pleasant places (e.g., a beach, swimming pool, forest, mountain scene, river, lake, park, or country view).

Take the first photo and look at it for about two minutes, trying to retain the complete image in your mind. Now turn the photo face-down, close your eyes, and imagine the scene for about two minutes. At this point just focus on what you can *see* (the *visual modality*).

O.K., now we'll ask you to do that again. Let's extend the image to include the *hearing modality*. That is, on this occasion, we want you to imagine not only what you can see but also what you can hear—as if you were taking the photo again. Just examine the photo for some clues of the sounds that you might be able to hear (e.g., birds chirping, water flowing, etc.). Now turn the photo facedown, close your eyes, and imagine the scene, complete with sight and hearing.

Now we'll ask you to do that yet again. On this occasion, we want you to imagine not only what you can see and hear but also what you can *smell*—as if you were taking the photo again. Just examine the photo for some clues of the smells that you might be able to detect if you were at the scene again. Now turn the photo facedown, close your eyes, and imagine the scene, complete with sight, hearing, and smell.

We'll ask you to do this exercise one more time. On this occasion, we want you to imagine not only what you can see, hear, and smell but also what you can imagine in another sense (*taste* and/or *touch*)—as if you were taking the photo again with all the richness of the original experience. Just examine the photo for some clues of the touch or taste sensations that you might be able to detect if you were there again. Don't worry if you can't find anything more to add to the scene. You may have selected one that cannot easily include another sense. Now turn the photo facedown, close your eyes, and imagine the scene, complete with all possible senses.

By now you are probably well on the way to refining your skill in imagery training. If you are having difficulty with these exercises, we suggest that you go back to the sensory modality that is easiest for you to use. Some people seem to be unable to develop images in all the senses. This phenomenon is perfectly normal, so don't worry if this applies to you. Many people can imagine the visual scenes more easily than the others.

If you have progressed well with this exercise, try taking the second photo and repeating the final version of the exercise with that photo (i.e., applying all the senses). You might be finding that this exercise is so much fun that you would like to devote some time to doing it on a regular basis. That is fine, but the main aim is to build up your imagery ability so that you can simply conjure up scenes whenever and wherever you wish to do so. We also ask you to think back on the period during which you have been doing this exercise. To what extent have you noticed the tinnitus? You might have noticed that it has faded into the background, only to be more obvious again now that we have drawn your attention to it! Perhaps this is an example of the foreground/background experience that we have previously described. People often report that their tinnitus fades into the background when they are involved in some task that requires more concentration.

## Exercise 5: Combining the Senses Using Favorite Pictures

In this exercise, we ask you to go through a magazine or examine an art book to look for photos or paintings that appeal to you. Take two or three of these items and spend some time doing the same exercise as you have just completed with the personal photos. Just imagine that you are actually in the scene, looking in a particular direction (e.g., from left to right, or from right to left, or into the distance). If there are people in the scene, you might imagine that you are one of those people. Take that person's perspective and imagine what you can see, hear, smell, taste, and touch. Go through this exercise with two or three photos or paintings.

## *Movement in Imagery*

The next step in developing your imagery ability is to imagine movement within the images. Perhaps you have already been incorporating movement (e.g., in the fireworks image). Here, we will focus specifically on developing movement imagery ability.

### Exercise 6: Movement Imagery Training

Imagine each of the following situations for about half a minute:

- A pendulum or seesaw
- A clock with the secondhand moving around its face
- Waves rolling onto a beach
- Trees blowing in the wind
- A kite flying in the air
- A bird flying in the air
- A fish swimming in a fishtank

- Someone playing a piano, guitar, or violin
- Watching a tennis game from a side-on position, right in line with the net (imagining the ball going back and forth across the net)
- (If you prefer another sport, try the same idea—a golf swing, football teams, etc.)
- An orchestra or group of musicians

## Some Suggested Scenes

Now let's try some more imagery exercises for practice. In the following section we describe four scenes. Work through these at your own pace. Read through each scene first and then close your eyes and try to visualize the scene in your mind's eye. Remember, using imagery techniques is a bit like daydreaming, except that you will control the process more. Some daydreams can be quite vivid; attempt to capture the image of the scenes in your mind as clearly as you can. Remember to incorporate as many sensory modalities as possible (e.g., sight, sounds, smell, touch, taste). The exercises will gradually introduce more sensory aspects as they unfold. Should you experience any difficulty, just try to go along with the suggested scene and try to imagine whatever aspects that you can.

### Exercise 7: Additional Imagery Training Exercises

#### *Exercise 7.1: The Beach*

Read the following scene and then close your eyes and try to capture the images in your mind:

> Imagine that you are at the beach. It is early morning. Try to visualize the sand, the beach, and the sea. Picture a wide sweep of fine, white, cool sand—see the pale sky and the sun just beginning to rise. Visualize the sea, notice how the waves

form—they roll quietly in, curl over, and then break. Each wave washes up the sand—notice the curves of soft creamy foam wash up the sand—and then see how the water recedes. Keep the waves forming, rolling quietly in, curling, breaking, and washing up the beach in curves of soft creamy foam—they form, roll, curl, break, and wash up the beach. Now, let the images fade away... fade away completely. Slowly open your eyes.

### Exercise 7.2: The Countryside

*Imagine that you are out in the countryside. You are sitting in the shade on a grassy bank overlooking a cool stream. Feel the grass beneath you. Although you are mostly shaded by the trees, you can feel the warm sun on your feet. You can feel the soft texture of the grass under the palms of your hands. You can see the stream full of clear water. The water is so clear that you can see the pebbles on the bottom. You can see the movement of the water in the stream as it runs over the pebbles. Try to visualize the scene. Imagine you are sitting there—see the tall trees around you—the branches of the trees all join above you, like a ceiling of leaves—this shades you but you can still see the sun, speckles of sunlight through the branches—feel the warmth on your feet. Imagine the coolness, visualize the stream—clear, cool water running over water-worn pebbles. The smell of the fresh green grass and the scent of wildflowers fills the air. You can hear the water running over the pebbles and hear birds chirping in the trees. Watch the pattern of the running water. Now visualize that you pick up a fallen leaf on the grass beside you and drop it into the water—the leaf hits the water and begins to bob, and float downstream. Watch the leaf float downstream and out of view. Imagine you pick up another leaf and drop it into the stream—watch it bob up and down, and float away downstream and out of view. Just for a few quiet moments imagine sitting on the grassy bank and continue to pick up leaves, one by one, and drop them into the stream—watch them bob and float away downstream and out of view... that's fine, now let all the images fade away and open your eyes. (Henry & Wilson, 2001).*

### Exercise 7.3: The Beach Revisited

Once again, imagine that you are at the beach. It is the middle of the day. Try to visualize the sand, the beach, and the sea. There is a wide sweep of fine, white sand and there is a bright blue sky. See the sun high in the sky. Visualize the sea, notice how the waves form—they roll quietly in, curl over, and then break. Each wave washes up the sand—notice the curves of soft creamy foam wash up the sand—and then see how the water recedes. Feel the warmth of the sun on your arms. You can hear birds flying overhead. You can hear people laughing as they swim, and the repetitive crashing of waves on the shore. Listen to the sound of the waves. The sun is pleasantly warm on your body—not too hot. What else can you see? What can you hear? Just try to capture the scene in your mind.... Now, let the images fade away... fade away completely. Slowly open your eyes.

### Exercise 7.4: The Log-Fire Experience

Imagine that you are sitting in front of a log fire in a comfortable room. It is the middle of winter. Looking out the window you can see that the entire landscape is covered with snow; it is completely white. Now picture the fire. The wood is burning bright. Feel the warmth on your body. Notice the colors of the embers as they burn—vibrant orange and red—smell the burning wood. Spend a few moments capturing all of these images in your mind. Notice how the wood makes a crackling sound as it burns. Feel the warmth as the fire warms the room. In your mind capture the warmth, the crackling sound of the fire, the color of the embers, the smell of the burning wood. And in a moment, reach over and in one hand pick up some of the roasted chestnuts placed on a plate on the table. Imagine the taste as you eat the still warm chestnuts. Enjoy the situation for a few moments while you capture all aspects of the moment. Then let the images slowly fade away. Now, slowly open your eyes.

These are just a few examples of some scenes that can be used to conjure up mental images. Of course, there are many other scenes that you could use—for example:

- If you enjoy fishing, imagine you are preparing for a trip. Plan what you need to take, picturing each item. Visualize yourself on the beach, on some rocks, or in a boat. What can you see? What can you smell? What can you hear? What can you feel? Have you got a bite?

- Imagine your last holiday, or a holiday you enjoyed some years ago. Recapture all of the memories in your mind. Imagine the sights you saw, the places you visited, the people you met, the meals you ate, the funny things that happened, the stories that you told when you got home!

In considering scenes that could be evoked via mental imagery, the list is endless. We will leave it up to you to think of some other scenes that might be especially pleasant for you. Be as creative as you like. Let's now focus on some imagery techniques in which the tinnitus is addressed more directly.

## *Imagery Techniques Incorporating Your Tinnitus*

The previous exercises were selected to allow you to practice the general principles of imagery training. In the following exercises you will be introduced to ways of incorporating your tinnitus into an image. It sounds weird, doesn't it? Try it and see how it goes—you have nothing to lose! We recommend that you read through and practice each of the following exercises to see which best suits you.

One way of incorporating your tinnitus into your imagery exercises is to build a scene around the type of sound which you experience. For example, a roaring tinnitus sound may be rather like the sound of the sea, a waterfall, a fountain, or a stream. Other sounds may be like insects in the trees or grass in summer, not especially enjoyable, but nevertheless a natural and familiar sound.

Think about the sound of your tinnitus and try to relate it to a natural external sound. Then try to imagine a situation in which your tinnitus sound is related to some sound in the environment. Remember to add all sensory experiences to the scene, including sight, smell, sound, and physical sensations so that you make the imagined scene as vivid and realistic as possible. Here are some suggestions that you may practice:

- *If the noise of your tinnitus sounds like ocean waves crashing, imagine that you are near the ocean and can hear the waves crashing. You can see the beach, see the golden sand, see the water; imagine the waves rolling in; smell the salt air; feel the warm sand under your feet—feel the cool water as you walk along the shore; smell the aroma of hot chips; hear the seagulls; watch the people swimming and surfing—as the waves roll and break on the shore.*
- *If the noise of your tinnitus sounds like a hissing kettle then imagine this is what it is. You can see the kettle sitting on the stove, the stove is lit—you can see the red coil or gas flame. Imagine you are making a cup of tea or coffee—imagine going through the process. Visualize yourself in the kitchen—you get the tea or coffee, you get the milk and sugar. Now what would be nice to eat with this?—some biscuits or cake—think of how much you are enjoying having a coffee or tea break, and eating your snack!*
- *If the noise of your tinnitus sounds like an electric fan then imagine this is what it is. Imagine you are sitting in a comfortable chair—it is a warm summer day, the fan is on and is blowing a cool breeze on you. Study the shape of the fan—notice how cool and pleasant you feel. Imagine that you reach out and pick up a cool refreshing drink—taste the drink, and sit back comfortably and enjoy the cool flow of air fanning your body!*
- *If the noise of your tinnitus sounds like insects then imagine this is what it is. Imagine it is a perfect summer evening, you can see the sun low in the sky—it is warm but not too hot. You can hear the insects but what else can you hear? Imagine you can hear birds whistling, you can see the leaves on the tree moving gently in the breeze—you can hear them gently rustling in the wind. What else can you see? What sensations can you feel on your skin? (Henry & Wilson, 2001)*

In one of our groups, one person said that he could imagine his tinnitus as the sound of a steak sizzling on the hot barbecue. Not everyone finds it easy to match their tinnitus sounds to external ones. Should you find it difficult to match the sound of your tinnitus to an external sound, it may be useful to imagine that your tinnitus is some other sound—a pleasant, soothing sound. Alternatively, some people find it useful to imagine some sound other than their tinnitus, but one that is pleasant, and that may be used imaginally, to mask their own tinnitus (e.g., the sound of a waterfall, a fountain, a particular piece of music). A further possibility is to focus sensory aspects of an imagined scene on to sensations other than sound— that is, to focus on smell, sight (especially color), taste, and touch modalities.

## *Conclusion*

There are a number of different ways of achieving attentional control. In this chapter we have described several methods. People tend to differ in terms of which method they prefer. We recommend that you "trial" each approach so that you can test the techniques and determine which ones work best for you. You will need to practice the techniques on a daily basis to build up your skill. Try to spend approximately 10 to 20 minutes each day practicing the exercises. You should feel free to experiment with the suggested techniques. Try to be creative and modify them to design strategies that effectively work for you. As your skill increases, we strongly recommend that you practice these self-control strategies in everyday situations whenever you find that you are aware of your tinnitus. Attention control and imagery techniques may be particularly useful for dealing with sleep difficulties or dealing with other "quiet" times of the day—times when there is little occurring around you to serve as a distraction from your tinnitus. By gaining greater control over your attentional processes, you can learn to change the way you react to tinnitus. This, in turn, will lead to less emotional distress.

# 8

# *Becoming Your Own Coach*

*After attending the group I found it really useful to just try to talk myself through any situations that I found difficult. Yes, I talk to myself! Never thought that I'd admit it, but I find it extremely useful! When I find myself in a difficult situation, or when I notice that my tinnitus is worse for some reason, I find myself saying something like, "O.K. This isn't good—you need to get things under control." I think over the techniques that I have been practicing and try to work out which ones might work for me, given the particular situation. For instance, if I'm feeling a bit uptight, I'll take a moment and do some relaxation exercises. This is like taking a bit of "time-out." Then I try to take stock of what it is that is bothering me. I ask myself: "What is it that is troubling me?" I did this just the other day. I was about to go to a meeting at work that I was worried about. I had really worked myself into a state! I felt tense, sweaty, hot, and my stomach was beginning to churn. So then I thought: "What are you doing to yourself? Just think things through—how do you want to deal with this?" I then started to work out a way of talking myself through the whole situation. I remembered how my baseball coach used to do this whenever our team had a problem in a game. So this is the way that I now approach my tinnitus—I try to act as my own coach!*

## *Using Self-Instructions*

In this book we have described a range of self-control strategies that can effectively lead you to change your response to tinnitus via your perceptual, emotional, and attentional processes. Some of these strategies may be used on their own, but the majority of them produce the most beneficial results when they are employed in conjunction with each other. Self-instructions may be regarded as a self-control method in which people "internally" give themselves "instructions." To put this more simply, you talk to yourself! Self-instructions can be used in combination with all the other skills that you have been taught in this book. Most importantly, they can be used as a reminder to employ and integrate the various self-control skills. That is, you can use them to become your own coach in the implementation of an effective course of action to manage problematic situations that give rise to tinnitus-related distress. The effective use of self-instructions involves a number of steps that you should follow prior to, during, and after a problem situation. These include the following:

1. *Prior to the Situation*
   This phase involves anticipating or preparing for a problem situation. In order to anticipate what you need to do to deal with a stressful tinnitus-related situation, ask yourself the questions:
   - What do I have to do to manage this situation in the way I want?
   - How would I be acting and thinking if I were handling the situation effectively?
   Then make a list of specific self-instructions about how to accomplish this.

2. *During the Situation*
   This step relates to the time period when you are actually handling the situation.
   Be your own coach—motivate and direct yourself about what to do when faced with an upsetting situation. Encourage

and direct yourself by specifically focusing on any upsetting feelings you may be experiencing. Check that you are thinking in a helpful way and remind yourself to use all of your self-control skills.

Use self-instructions that highlight your ability to control tinnitus and counteract your worry about inability to cope.

**3.** *After You Have Handled the Situation*
This step is particularly important. You need to acknowledge your success in managing a situation. Even if the situation did not go as well as you might have liked, you need to recognize and reward your efforts for trying. You can then take some time to plan how your efforts could be improved next time.

Use the same skills to evaluate how you handled the situation once the event is over. Use self-instructions to reward yourself for success. Remember that "success" includes dealing with a challenge to the best of your ability. Identify what you have learned for the next time you encounter a similar situation. Develop new and encouraging self instructions for the future.

The process described in steps 1 to 3 are illustrated in Figure 8.1.

It is useful for you to have a cue to remind you to use, or "switch on," your self-instructional statements. For example, you could use the presence of negative or unhelpful thoughts as such a cue, or the fact that you are worrying about some forthcoming event that you fear might exacerbate your tinnitus. Figure 8.2 presents a general and tinnitus-specific example of how negative thoughts might be used as a cue to employ self-instructions.

Of course, you will need to develop a set of self-instructions that are tailor-made to suit yourself. The same set of instructions will not be equally helpful for all people. You should choose self-instructions that are brief, easily remembered, believable, genuine, and personally relevant. Self-instructional statements can be used to help you analyze and alter negative thoughts. For example, when you notice that you are thinking in a negative, or unconstructive fashion, you might use the following self-instructions:

**FIGURE 8.1**  *An Example of How to Use Self-Instructional Statements*

---

**A** = Situation

1.  *Noticing the Tinnitus*
    - View the tinnitus as a problem that you can do something about.
      — *"What is it I have to do?"*
      — *"I can develop a plan to deal with it."*
    - Prepare yourself by making a plan or mental outline of how you will deal with the sensations when they arise.
      — *"Just think about what I have to do."*
    - Focus on what the situation requires—focus on the present.
    - Review *all* the strategies that you know and that may be helpful.
      — *"Think of the things that I can use to help me control the tinnitus."*
      — *"Don't worry; worry won't help anything."*
      — *"I could just pause for a moment and relax, then I'll develop a plan—a bit of problem solving might also be useful."*
    - Use any anxiety or worry as a reminder or cue to focus on what you have to do.
      — *"Remember, I can shift my attention to anything I want to. My attention does not have to be stuck on the tinnitus—let's shift the focus to something else."*
    - Remind and reassure yourself that you are able to use various self-control strategies. Remember your thoughts and attention are under your control.

2.  *Confronting the Tinnitus*
    - View the tinnitus as a challenge—do not view it as a disaster.
      — *"I can deal with the tinnitus as a challenge—I can challenge it and not let it overwhelm me."*
      — *"One step at a time, I can handle the tinnitus; it's not pleasant but I can handle it."*
    - Don't do everything at once—don't be overwhelmed. Rather, develop a logical plan, using each of the self-control skills you have learned.
      — *"Take a deep breath in, let it out and relax. Just pause for a moment."*
      — *"I won't think about the tinnitus. I'll just focus on what I have to do—the task at hand, focus on what I can do right now to help me deal with the situation."*

3.  *Managing Thoughts and Feelings at Critical Moments*
    (This refers to times when you notice that the intensity of the tinnitus seems to be increasing, or when you think that you can't manage any more.)
    - Keep in mind the task at hand—focus on what you have to do.
      — *"When I notice the tinnitus, I just pause and keep focusing on what I have to do."*
    - Be realistic. You are not trying to eliminate the tinnitus—but you can take control.
      — *"The tinnitus may be present but I can keep it at a manageable level. Don't overreact, that will make things worse. Just try to keep your focus of attention on the task at hand—that way, the tinnitus may merge into the background."*

**FIGURE 8.1** *Continued*

---

*—"Don't magnify the intensity of the sensations; don't catastrophize—that will only make things worse."*

*—"Remember, there are lots of things I can do; I can keep things under control."*

*—"Just pause, don't make things worse. I can review my plan of strategies— what can I switch to, what else can I do to make myself feel better?"*

- Consider using all of the various self-control skills: thought-stopping techniques, challenging thoughts, relaxation, attention control, and imagery skills.

4. *Self-Reflection and Positive Self-Statements*
   Throughout the three phases outlined above, it may be useful to evaluate your performance. You could use self-instructions, or self-statements such as:
   - *"How am I doing?"*
   - *"That worked pretty well!"*

   Remember, people often criticize themselves, but rarely praise their behavior. Throughout a stressful situation, evaluate how you are doing. This will help you keep on task. If you feel you should be doing better, you can use this as a cue to try different strategies. Most importantly, acknowledge that you are using your self-control skills and give yourself a "pat on the back" for doing so. Some examples might include:
   - *"I'm doing pretty well, it's not as hard as I thought!"*
   - *"I'm doing better all the time!"*
   - *"I won't let negative thoughts interfere with my plan."*
   - *"I knew I could handle it—I'm doing pretty well!"*
   - *"Each time I practice the self-management strategies I get better at using them."*

---

*Source:* Henry & Wilson, 2001

Slow down, stop jumping to conclusions, check out all the possibilities, think of alternatives. What's really true here? What facts might I be overlooking?

You might also use self-instructional statements as a reminder to employ all your self-control techniques, including relaxation, attention control, imagery, and thought-stopping skills. Some people find that self-instructional statements work best if they address themselves by their own name when using them. Try using your own name and see if that helps.

**FIGURE 8.2**    *Using Negative Thoughts as a Cue to Use Self-Instructions*

| General Example | Tinnitus Example |
|---|---|
| **A = Situation** | **A = Situation** |
| *Bill is going to talk to his boss about the possibility of a raise.* | *Bill suffers from tinnitus and is attending a social function at a local busy restaurant.* |
| **B = Negative Thoughts** | **B = Negative Thoughts** |
| *"What if the boss gets mad? What if I can't say anything when I walk into his office? What if I just freeze?* | *"How can I enjoy myself at this dinner? What if my tinnitus is especially loud when I get home?"* |
| *"Switch on" self-instructions* | *"Switch on" self-instructions* |
| *"STOP."* | *"STOP."* |
| *"These thoughts are just getting me scared. Take a breath, think of what you're going to say: 'I want to talk to you about getting a raise.' Good, that's what I'll say."* | *"These thoughts are just getting me upset. I haven't even eaten my meal yet. Who's to say my tinnitus will be loud when I get home. Just focus on the present—forget the tinnitus. I just want to enjoy this dinner."* |

*Source:* Henry & Wilson, 2001

# Self-Assessment Exercise 13: Developing Personalized Self-Instructions

Figure 8.3 presents an illustration of how self-instructions might be applied to tinnitus. Read through this example and then complete Self-Assessment Exercise 13 described in Figure 8.4.

# Problem-Solving Training

Having to manage problematic situations is a normal aspect of daily living. In this section we will describe problem-solving training—a method designed to provide you with a general strategy for coping

**FIGURE 8.3** *A Tinnitus-Related Example of How to Use Self-Instructions*

---

**A** = Situation

Jim is attending a social function at a local restaurant

1. *Preparing for the Situation*
   *"O.K., I know I get a bit concerned about going to social functions now that I have tinnitus—but I can develop a plan to deal with this. No negative self-statements or thoughts, just think clearly and rationally. It'll be good to get out and celebrate. I can spend the next hour or so before I go just doing something pleasant—don't think about the tinnitus."*

2. *Confronting and Dealing with the Situation*
   *"One step at a time—don't think about the tinnitus or whether it'll be loud when I get home. No need to think about that—that'll surely just make it worse. Just focus on the here and now. If I use all of my self-control strategies I know I can deal with it. I'll just remember to use my relaxation skills, watch my thinking, and use my attention control skills."*

3. *Dealing with the Situation if Feelings Increase*
   *"It's quite noisy here and a bit difficult to hear what people are saying. But it's O.K.; the food and company are good. If you don't quite understand what people are saying, just ask them to repeat themselves. No point in thinking about how my tinnitus will be later. Even if it does seem louder when I get home that's O.K.; that will only be temporary and it'll settle back down. One good thing now is that because of all the background noise it's rather difficult to hear my tinnitus. Now let's get my attention off the tinnitus—focus it back on to the celebrations."*

4. *Reinforcing Self-Statements When Situation Is Over*
   *"It worked—I was able to keep my emotions and feelings under control. Even though social situations are not that easy now that I have the tinnitus, I didn't let it spoil the evening. My negative thoughts are a large part of the problem. If I think I won't cope or won't enjoy something—or it will affect my tinnitus, it usually does. This time I just let the tinnitus be there without focusing on it—I kept my attention on the celebrations, the food, and company. This experience will help me practice the self-instructions again in the future. They certainly helped to keep me focused on all the new self-control skills I have—that was a job well done!"*

---

*Source:* Henry & Wilson, 2001

**FIGURE 8.4    *Self-Assessment Exercise 13:*
*Developing Personalized Self-Instructions***

---

The aim of this exercise is to help you begin to use the self-instructional technique to manage difficulties associated with tinnitus. Anticipate challenging situations, plan effective strategies, verbalize encouraging self-instructional statements, and give yourself praise for your efforts at the end. Also, use the self-instruction statements to remind yourself to use all your self-control techniques (thought challenging, thought stopping, relaxation, attention control, imagery skills, etc.). To begin this practice, identify one specific stressful situation related to your tinnitus and make a list of self-instructional statements tailor-made to assist you in dealing with this particular situation. Please complete the following:

   1. *Identify a Specific Stressful Situation*
      Examples may include getting to sleep, going to a social engagement, concentrating on some task or activity, trying to relax, being in a quiet environment, being in a noisy environment, having a conversation in a noisy situation, concentrating on reading or on watching television, having dinner in a restaurant, or having a conversation on the telephone.

      *One specific stressful situation for me is:*

      _____

      _____


   2. *List Your Self-Instructional Statements*
      2.1: List some self-instructional statements you could use when *preparing for* the situation.

      _____

      _____

      _____


      2.2: List some self-instructional statements you could use for coping *when feelings start to build:*

      _____

      _____

      _____

**FIGURE 8.4** *Continued*

---

2.3: List some self-instructional statements you could use for coping *when feelings start to overwhelm:*

_____

_____

_____

2.4: List some self-instructional statements you could use for coping *when the situation is over:*

_____

_____

_____

---

*Source:* Henry & Wilson, 2001

with problems. The goal of problem-solving training is not to offer you specific solutions to specific situations, but rather to teach you a general framework to use in solving a diverse range of problems (i.e., current and future problems). By learning effective problem-solving skills you will be in a better position to manage a variety of problems. Problem solving can actually be fun! You will feel a sense of accomplishment when you achieve control of some problem situations.

The key components of problem solving are outlined in Figure 8.5. An illustrative example of how this approach might be applied to a specific tinnitus-related problem is shown in Figure 8.6.

## Self-Assessment Exercise 14: Practicing Problem Solving

Read through the steps involved in problem solving in Figure 8.5 and then the example provided in Figure 8.6. Then complete the

## FIGURE 8.5  *Steps in Problem Solving*

**Step 1:** Take a breather—pause while you decide what to do.

**Step 2:** Ask yourself: *"What is the problem—What am I trying to change?"* Be specific!

**Step 3:** Ask yourself: *"How can I solve this problem—What are the options?"*
- Write down as many possible solutions that you can think of.
- Think of how a friend might approach the problem.

**Step 4:** Ask yourself: *"What way will work best for me in this situation?"*
- Try to identify which of the many possible solutions that you identified at step 3 might best address the problem. Select a solution from your list.

**Step 5:** Try the selected way of dealing with the problem.

**Step 6:** Ask yourself: *"How did it go? How well has it worked? What can I learn from this for next time?"*
- If the problem is resolved, praise yourself for your efforts.
- If the problem is unresolved, praise yourself for at least attempting to resolve it; then go back to steps 4 and 5 and select an alternative solution.

*Source:* Henry & Wilson, 2001

## FIGURE 8.6  *How to Apply Problem-Solving to a Tinnitus-Related Problem*

### Step 1: Take a Breath.
*"O.K. I'll just spend a few moments practicing some relaxation."*

### Step 2: Identify the Specific Problem.
*"There are so many questions I want to ask my doctor about my tinnitus, but I'm not sure how. He always seems so busy and there never seems to be enough time."*

### Step 3: Generate Solutions.
*"Now how can I solve this problem? I'll write down as many solutions as I can think of (good and poor):*
- *Ask the doctor for some reading material on tinnitus.*
- *Go to the library or buy a book on tinnitus.*
- *Take my partner with me so he/she can ask the questions.*
- *Write down my questions in a letter and mail them to my doctor.*
- *Find another doctor.*
- *When I go into his room I could explain to my doctor that I have some questions about my tinnitus that I'd like him to answer for me. I could take them written down on paper and hand them to the doctor.*

**FIGURE 8.6** *Continued*

---

- *Ask the receptionist to schedule my appointment at a time when my doctor is not so busy.*
- *Just don't do anything.*
- *Explain to the receptionist that I have some questions I want to ask the doctor and get the receptionist's advice about how I should go about this.*
- *Tell my doctor off because he/she doesn't give me the information that I need.*
- *Ask my partner to go to the doctor and ask the questions for me."*

**Step 4: Select a Solution.**
*"O.K. I think I'll try just explaining that I have some questions about my tinnitus that I'd like the doctor to answer for me. I'll write a few down and hand them to him/her."*

**Step 5: Implement Solution.**
*Try the selected way of dealing with the problem.*

**Step 6: Reflect and Reward.**
Example, if problem resolved: *"O.K. All that trouble over nothing. I think I understand things better. There are a few other things I have thought about, but I'll ask about them next time. It was much better writing them down. I think that really helped. I managed that problem really well."*

Example, if problem unresolved: *"O.K. So things didn't go quite as I planned, but at least I attempted to solve the problem. I'll just go back to my list and select another possible solution. Then I'll give it another go."*

---

Self-Assessment Exercise (Parts A and B) described in Figures 8.7 and 8.8 to begin practicing applying problem-solving techniques.

## *Conclusion*

In this chapter we have described two additional cognitive (thought-management) methods: self-instructions and problem solving. Self-instructions can be used to help "talk" yourself through a difficult or stressful situation. They can also be used to help you to integrate all of the self-control strategies that we have introduced you to in the earlier chapters. Developing personalized self-statements can assist you in remaining focused on some difficult task, or be applied on those occasions when you are troubled by your tinnitus.

### FIGURE 8.7 *Self-Assessment Exercise 14 (Part A): Practicing Problem Solving*

This exercise is designed to provide you with some practice in applying problem solving. We have specified a problem at Step 2. Try to imagine that a friend has come to you complaining of this problem:

- How could you help your friend to work through the various steps that are involved in problem solving?
- How might you help your friend solve this problem?

**Step 1:** Take a breather—pause while you decide what to do.

**Step 2:** The problem is: Your friend has recently come home from the hospital after having surgery. When she was in the hospital she received a lot of visitors and cards wishing her all the best. Now that she is home she is feeling lonely and isolated.

**Step 3:** Generate some possible solutions.
Write down as many possible solutions you can think of (good and poor).

_____

_____

_____

_____

_____

_____

**Step 4:** Select a solution.
Try to choose which of the many possible solutions that you identified at Step 3 might best address the problem. Select a solution from your list.

_____

_____

**Step 5:** Try the selected way of dealing with the problem.

**FIGURE 8.7** *Continued*

**Step 6:** Evaluate the problem-solving outcome
What would you suggest that your friend might say to herself afterward if the problem has been resolved?

_____

_____

What might you suggest that your friend say to herself afterward should the problem not be resolved?

_____

_____

_____

**FIGURE 8.8** *Self-Assessment Exercise 14 (Part B):*
*Practicing Problem-Solving*

In this exercise try to identify a problem that is troubling you. Be as specific as possible. Follow the steps in Figure 8.5 and begin to practice applying this approach to tinnitus-related problems.

**Step 1:** Take a breather—pause.

**Step 2:** Specify the problem.
*"One tinnitus-related problem for me is:"*

_____

_____

**Step 3:** Generate some possible solutions (good and poor).
*"How can I solve this problem? What are some of my options?"*

_____

_____

**FIGURE 8.8**  *Continued*

---

_____

_____

_____

_____

_____

_____

_____

_____

**Step 4:** Select one solution from your list.
*"What will work best for me in this situation?"*

_____

_____

**Step 5:** Try the selected way of dealing with the problem.

**Step 6:** Evaluate how things went and praise yourself for your efforts.
*"How did it go? How well did it work?"*

_____

_____

_____

_____

_____

The problem-solving techniques represent an all-purpose method of dealing with a wide range of problematic situations. You might find it useful to incorporate the two techniques of self-instructions and problem solving. For example, if you find that you need to deal with a particular problem (tinnitus-related or a more general problem), once you have specified the problem, made a list of solutions, and then decided on the best solution, you could also make a list of self-instructions to guide you in the process of actually implementing the solution. These two techniques can further equip you with a powerful means of taking control over your tinnitus. They can also be used to deal with high-risk situations, which is the focus of the next chapter.

# 9

## Dealing with High-Risk Situations

*Over the years I've learned that some situations are more difficult than others. When I'm tired I find it more difficult to cope with everything, especially my tinnitus. So when I haven't had sufficient sleep, or when things have been very hectic, I have to be more careful. Otherwise, I just don't cope with the usual demands that are placed on me! I have also noticed that my tinnitus troubles me more whenever I am experiencing some sort of stress in my life. For example, if I'm worried about work, my family, money, or my future, I find that I really notice the roaring sound in my left ear. At these times I really get quite distressed!*

## What Are High-Risk Situations?

High-risk situations are any circumstances that put you at risk of experiencing a worsening of tinnitus-related distress. These situations might include the occurrence of unpleasant life events, alterations in your emotional state, or periodic changes in audiological aspects of your tinnitus (e.g., increases in loudness). Typically, high-risk situations place a greater burden on your coping resources, and can undermine your ability to manage your tinnitus. They are quite likely to result in an increase in tinnitus-related difficulties (e.g., sleep problems, negative emotions such as feelings of tension or depression, social avoidance). In this chapter we will teach you how to learn to identify and prepare for high-risk situations. Preparation involves developing a specific plan of action that can be used at the time when the event occurs.

## *Negative Life Events and Tinnitus*

High-risk situations might arise from a variety of unpleasant events ranging from day-to-day hassles (e.g., misplacing your keys, being stuck in traffic) to more major life events (e.g., being laid off work, buying a new home). You might be aware of some adverse events directly related to your tinnitus (e.g., noisy places, lack of understanding from your partner). Unpleasant events that are unrelated to your tinnitus may also undermine your ability to cope with the tinnitus. For example, if you experience a failure in some project, or a bereavement, you might be at a higher risk of failing to manage your tinnitus effectively. It is also quite likely that you may be simultaneously at risk for developing symptoms of depression. In Figure 9.1 we present a model that might assist you in understanding the role of life events in relation to tinnitus.

Let's consider a few examples of the connection between life events and tinnitus. A person might experience some adverse life event, such as being laid off from work, which may give rise to feelings of depression. The more depressed the person becomes, the more difficult the individual might find it to use his or her self-control strategies (despite the fact that this is a time when the person certainly needs to!). Feelings of depression can tend to make a person view everything in a negative light, and as the feelings of depression increase, the person might perceive his or her tinnitus to become louder. This, in turn, might make the individual feel more annoyed and increasingly distressed. As more attention is focused on the tinnitus, it is likely that the person will begin to engage in negative thoughts in response to the tinnitus that will produce heightened levels of distress. A vicious cycle can easily emerge.

**FIGURE 9.1**   *The Role of Life Events in Relation to Tinnitus*

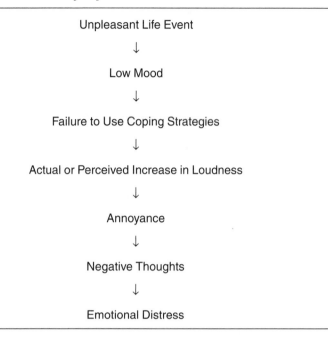

Unpleasant Life Event

↓

Low Mood

↓

Failure to Use Coping Strategies

↓

Actual or Perceived Increase in Loudness

↓

Annoyance

↓

Negative Thoughts

↓

Emotional Distress

Alternatively, a person might experience some actual change in his or her tinnitus. For instance, the person might be exposed to some form of noise that causes the tinnitus to become louder. In response to this situation, the person might fail to employ the self-control strategies (once again, at precisely the time when these would be indicated!). The individual might begin to engage in negative thoughts in response to the tinnitus—a sequence that is likely to produce feelings of depression and helplessness, as well as disruptions to social, leisure, and work activities, and that ultimately may lead to greater tinnitus-related distress.

High-risk situations vary from one person to another. It is important for you to learn to recognize the particular situations that might be problematic for you. Once you have identified these situations you can then begin to prepare some specific plans for dealing with them should they arise in the future.

## *Self-Assessment Exercises 15 and 16: Identifying High-Risk Situations*

From our experience, high-risk situations might include those described in Figure 9.2. For each situation we describe some specific example. In the space provided, try to write down at least one specific example for each type of situation.

Once you have worked through this exercise, complete Self-Assessment Exercises 15 and 16 described in Figures 9.3 and 9.4. In Self-Assessment Exercise 15, we ask you to complete the Tinnitus

**FIGURE 9.2    *Examples of High-Risk Situations***

- A stressful event that is caused by the tinnitus
  (e.g., difficulty hearing a conversation in a noisy room, _____)

- A stressful event that is not caused by tinnitus
  (e.g., running late, serious financial problems, _____)

- A social event
  (e.g., a crowded party, _____)

- Not having tinnitus understood by others
  (e.g., being told you're imagining it, _____)

- Events that produce lowering of mood
  (e.g., work-related stress, _____)

- Being in a noisy place for a long period
  (e.g., construction site, _____)

- Being exposed to a sudden loud noise
  (e.g., explosion, _____)

- Being in a quiet place
  (e.g., lying in bed, _____)

- Sleep problems
  (e.g., trouble falling asleep, _____)

**FIGURE 9.3** *Self-Assessment Exercise 15:*
*Tinnitus Self-Efficacy Questionnaire*

---

### Tinnitus Self-Efficacy Questionnaire

*Instructions*
A number of tasks are listed in this questionnaire. Please read each one carefully. Rate how confident you are that you can deal with each task despite your tinnitus *in the next week*. Write down a number from the scale below that best describes your degree of confidence.

0 ___ 10 ___ 20 ___ 30 ___ 40 ___ 50 ___ 60___ 70 ___ 80 ___ 90 ___ 100
Can't do it                Moderately confident        Extremely confident

The following are two examples unrelated to tinnitus:

**Example 1:**

| | Confidence |
|---|---|
| I can walk for at least 30 minutes each day. | 100 |
| I can walk for at least 1 hour each day. | 80 |
| I can walk for at least 2 hours each day. | 40 |
| I can walk for at least 4 hours each day. | 10 |

The answers indicate that I am extremely confident (rating = 100) that I can walk for at least 30 minutes a day in the next week.

**Example 2:**

| | Confidence |
|---|---|
| I can swim for at least half a lap at a time in an Olympic-sized swimming pool. | 90 |
| I can swim for at least 1 lap at a time in an Olympic-sized swimming pool. | 60 |
| I can swim for at least 2 laps at a time in an Olympic-sized swimming pool. | 30 |
| I can swim for at least 4 laps at a time in an Olympic-sized swimming pool. | 0 |

*Continued*

**FIGURE 9.3** *Continued*

---

The answers indicate that I am very confident (rating = 90) that I can swim at least half a lap at a time in the next week, and I am fairly confident (rating = 60) I can swim for at least 1 lap at a time. However, I am not very confident (rating = 30) I can swim for at least 2 laps at a time, and I don't think at all I can swim for at least 4 laps at a time in the coming week (rating = 0).

Now please complete all the items using the rating scale.

**Remember:** Rate your confidence that you can do the tasks despite your tinnitus *in the next week*. Please make sure you answer *every* item.

*Confidence*

I can become extremely relaxed for at least 15 minutes each day.        _____

I can become extremely relaxed for at least 30 minutes each day.        _____

I can become extremely relaxed for at least 1 hour each day.        _____

I can become extremely relaxed for at least 2 hours each day.        _____

I can fall asleep within 2 hours on most nights.        _____

I can fall asleep within 1 hour on most nights.        _____

I can fall asleep within 30 minutes on most nights.        _____

I can fall asleep within 15 minutes on most nights.        _____

I can follow conversation almost all the time when talking to 1–2 persons.        _____

I can follow conversation almost all the time when talking to 3–4 persons.        _____

I can follow conversation almost all the time when talking to 6–8 persons.        _____

I can follow conversation almost all the time when talking to 10–12 persons.        _____

I can distract myself from the tinnitus for at least 30 minutes each day.        _____

I can distract myself from the tinnitus for at least 1 hour each day.        _____

**FIGURE 9.3**  *Continued*

*Confidence*

I can distract myself from the tinnitus for at least
2 hours each day.

_____

I can distract myself from the tinnitus for at least
4 hours each day.

_____

When the tinnitus is very loud I can almost always keep
myself from being bothered by it for at least 30 minutes.

_____

When the tinnitus is very loud I can almost always keep
myself from being bothered by it for at least 1 hour.

_____

When the tinnitus is very loud I can almost always keep
myself from being bothered by it for at least 2 hours.

_____

When the tinnitus is very loud I can almost always keep
myself from being bothered by it for at least 4 hours.

_____

I can stay in a quiet situation without getting distressed
for at least 30 minutes each day.

_____

I can stay in a quiet situation without getting distressed
for at least 1 hour each day.

_____

I can stay in a quiet situation without getting distressed
for at least 2 hours each day.

_____

I can stay in a quiet situation without getting distressed
for at least 4 hours each day.

_____

I can keep myself from getting depressed because
of the tinnitus for at least 1 day this week.

_____

I can keep myself from getting depressed because
of the tinnitus for at least 3 days this week.

_____

I can keep myself from getting depressed because
of the tinnitus for at least 5 days this week.

_____

I can keep myself from getting depressed because
of the tinnitus everyday this week.

_____

*Continued*

**FIGURE 9.3** *Continued*

---

*Confidence*

When the tinnitus is very loud I can concentrate
(e.g., on reading, sewing, mental work, etc.) for
at least 30 minutes at a time.                                    _____

When the tinnitus is very loud I can concentrate
for at least 1 hour at a time.                                    _____

When the tinnitus is very loud I can concentrate
for at least 2 hours at a time.                                   _____

When the tinnitus is very loud I can concentrate
for at least 4 hours at a time.                                   _____


I can stay in a noisy situation (e.g., noisy cafeteria)
without getting distressed for at least 30 minutes each day.      _____

I can stay in a noisy situation without getting distressed
for at least 1 hour each day.                                     _____

I can stay in a noisy situation without getting distressed
for at least 2 hours each day.                                    _____

I can stay in a noisy situation without getting distressed
for at least 4 hours each day.                                    _____

---

*Source:* Henry & Wilson, 2001; developed by Aug, Kavanagh, & Wilson, 1991

**FIGURE 9.4** *Self-Assessment Exercise 16:
Identifying Your High-Risk Situations*

---

In order to identify personally relevant high-risk situations, you need to ask yourself: *To what type of situation am I most vulnerable?* This question may be partially addressed by self-monitoring of tinnitus distress, mood, and environmental situations that we introduced you to in Chapter 3. We suggest that you refer to your self-monitoring records to identify those situations or events that most affected the loudness of your tinnitus or the amount of tinnitus-related distress that you experience.

Next, refer to your responses to the Tinnitus Self-Efficacy Questionnaire that you completed in Figure 9.3. Check for any items that you rated as 40 or less. These represent situations in which you do not feel very confident, and thus are potential high-risk situations for you.

**FIGURE 9.4** *Continued*

Now, in the space provided, list the high-risk situations that are most problematic for you.

*My high-risk situations include:*

_____

_____

_____

_____

_____

_____

_____

Self-Efficacy Questionnaire. This will help you rate your level of self-efficacy (i.e., confidence) to deal with a range of situations despite your tinnitus. Any situations that receive a low confidence rating might represent high-risk situations for you. Self-Assessment Exercise 16 is designed to help you identify any other high-risk situations that are specifically relevant to you.

# *Self-Assessment Exercise 17: Prediction of Problematic Events*

A further strategy that might be useful in identifying and preparing for high-risk situations is the prediction of future negative life-events. In Figure 9.5 we describe Self-Assessment Exercise 17 in which we ask you to complete the Life Events Prediction Questionnaire. This questionnaire asks you to predict the likelihood of the occurrence of 30 events, and to rate how confident you are that you could deal with each event if it should occur.

**FIGURE 9.5** *Self-Assessment Exercise 17: Life Events Prediction Questionnaire*

---

### Life Events Prediction Questionnaire

This questionnaire contains a list of events or situations that commonly occur in people's lives. You may have had experience with one or more of these events, either recently or at some time in the past. We are interested in identifying those events that you think might occur in the future—specifically in the next *year.* We are also interested to know how confident you are that you can deal with the event if it were to occur within the next year. You can rate each event on two scales. The first scale simply asks for your rating of the likelihood that the event will occur.

Rate the likelihood on a scale from 0 (extremely *unlikely* to occur) to 100 (highly *likely* to occur). You can simply *write on the line* the number that best reflects your estimation about the likely occurrence of the event.

| 0 | 10 | 20 | 30 | 40 | 50 | 60 | 70 | 80 | 90 | 100 |
|---|----|----|----|----|----|----|----|----|----|-----|
| Extremely |||||||||| Highly |
| unlikely |||||||||| likely |
| to occur |||||||||| to occur |

---

Then we ask you to rate *how confident you are that you can deal with the event* in an effective way if it does occur *without receiving any professional help.*

You can rate the confidence on a scale from 0 (not very confident that you can deal with it) to 100 (very confident that you can deal with it). This number can be written on the second line.

| 0 | 10 | 20 | 30 | 40 | 50 | 60 | 70 | 80 | 90 | 100 |
|---|----|----|----|----|----|----|----|----|----|-----|
| Not very |||||||||| Very |
| confident |||||||||| confident |
| that I can |||||||||| that I can |
| deal with it |||||||||| deal with it |

---

Please rate the *confidence* level even if you judge that the event is not likely to occur. Ask yourself, "Well, if it *did occur,* how confident am I that I can deal with it without professional help?"

**FIGURE 9.5** *Continued*

Now here are the items: ***Please place a number from 0 to 100 on each line.***

| | Likelihood of occurrence | Confidence in dealing with it |
|---|---|---|
| 1. Serious or continuing problems with the behavior of children in your care | _____ | _____ |
| 2. Your working conditions deteriorate (including home duties), e.g., more tedious or boring tasks, poorer physical conditions, longer hours, inadequate job recognition | _____ | _____ |
| 3. You frequently have things break or not run properly | _____ | _____ |
| 4. Frequent transport problems develop | _____ | _____ |
| 5. You have several minor illnesses or injuries | _____ | _____ |
| 6. Prolonged separation from your close partner | _____ | _____ |
| 7. Break-up of a romantic relationship or divorce | _____ | _____ |
| 8. You are demoted; you change jobs for a worse one; or you do not receive an expected promotion | _____ | _____ |
| 9. You have a serious accident (or several minor accidents) | _____ | _____ |
| 10. You become unemployed, sacked, or laid off work | _____ | _____ |
| 11. Something that you value greatly is stolen, lost, or severely damaged | _____ | _____ |
| 12. You experience a significant increase in demands or obligations at work or home | _____ | _____ |

*Continued*

**FIGURE 9.5** *Continued*

|  | Likelihood of occurrence | Confidence in dealing with it |
|---|---|---|
| 13. Serious or frequent problems in a relationship with someone at work develop (e.g., arguments, taunting, "freezing" you out, unpleasant interaction with boss, etc.) | _____ | _____ |
| 14. Serious or frequent problems with neighbors | _____ | _____ |
| 15. You have problems with alcohol or other drugs | _____ | _____ |
| 16. You have a serious or prolonged health problem other than tinnitus (from illness or injury) | _____ | _____ |
| 17. Death of an immediate family member or close friend | _____ | _____ |
| 18. Someone close to you develops problems with alcohol or other drugs | _____ | _____ |
| 19. Someone close to you develops psychiatric problems | _____ | _____ |
| 20. Your living arrangements (accommodation) become unsatisfactory | _____ | _____ |
| 21. You have legal problems (e.g., difficulties with the police, a civil law suit, real estate problems) | _____ | _____ |
| 22. You have serious or frequent disagreements or arguments with someone with whom you have previously been on good terms | _____ | _____ |
| 23. You or your close partner have problems relating to pregnancy or childbirth (e.g., abortion, miscarriage, unwanted pregnancy, or you discover that you cannot have children) | _____ | _____ |
| 24. Your social situation changes so that you are more frequently alone or do not have people around you who share your interests | _____ | _____ |

**FIGURE 9.5**  *Continued*

|  | Likelihood of occurrence | Confidence in dealing with it |
|---|---|---|
| 25. You have a failure on an important examination (assignment) or a major task or business venture | _____ | _____ |
| 26. You experience sexual or other relationship difficulties | _____ | _____ |
| 27. Prolonged separation from a close friend or immediate family member (or severely reduced contact with them) | _____ | _____ |
| 28. You fail to gain entry to a course which you wished to undertake | _____ | _____ |
| 29. You run into financial difficulties | _____ | _____ |
| 30. Someone close to you develops a serious illness or has a serious injury | _____ | _____ |

*Source:* Henry & Wilson 2001; developed by Kavanagh & Wilson, 1987

# *Preparation for High-Risk Situations*

It is a simple fact of life that you might encounter high-risk situations from time to time. However, with adequate preparation you can become more confident that you will be equipped to deal with such situations. This preparation requires that you develop recognition and response skills in relation to high-risk situations. *Recognition skills* mean that you are able to see that there is a difficulty when it arises (i.e., you can identify high-risk situations). *Response skills* means that you have a repertoire of coping strategies to draw upon in order to handle these problem situations (i.e., you have a plan of action). The self-instructional strategy that we described in Chapter 8 might be an especially useful technique to help you to meet the demands imposed by any high-risk event. Of course, not all events are predictable, so not all events can receive preparation in this way. You will also need a general way of handling unpredictable problematic situations. The problem-solving skills that we described in Chapter 8 can be a way of accomplishing this goal.

## *Self-Assessment Exercises 18 to 21: Developing Plans to Deal with High-Risk Situations*

Now let's use some of the material that you have identified in Self-Assessment Exercises 15, 16, and 17 as the basis for developing strategies to effectively deal with problematic high-risk situations or life events should they arise in the future. One aspect of being prepared for these events is that you have developed a plan beforehand. It is preferable that such plans be written down so that they can be retrieved easily should the event actually occur. Self-Assessment Exercises 18 to 21 are described in Figures 9.6, 9.7, 9.8, and 9.9. These exercises are designed to help you to begin to develop response skills that will enable you to be prepared for high-risk situations that might arise in the future.

**FIGURE 9.6  *Self-Assessment Exercise 18:
Preparing for High-Risk Situations***

Select *one* of the high-risk situations that you identified in Self-Assessment Exercise 16 (Figure 9.4). Now try to identify how you might respond to the event, by answering the questions listed below. Through this process you can begin to develop a plan for dealing with this event should it arise in the future.

• *One example of a high-risk situation that is problematic for me is:*

_____

_____

• *How could this come about (i.e., under what circumstances)?*

_____

**FIGURE 9.6** *Continued*

_____

_____

_____

• *When is this most likely to occur?*

_____

_____

_____

• *Why? How do I know?*

_____

_____

_____

• *What can I do, if anything, to prevent this from happening?* (Draw up a list of possible steps to prevent the occurrence of the event.)

_____

_____

_____

• *Has something like this ever happened before? (If yes: When? What happened? How did I cope with it?)*

_____

_____

_____

*Continued*

**FIGURE 9.6** *Continued*

---

- *What were the negative consequences?*

_____

_____

_____

_____

- *Were there any positive consequences?*

_____

_____

_____

_____

- *If this does happen, what will be its effect on me on this occasion? How might I think in response to the event? How might I feel in response to the event?*

_____

_____

_____

- *What do I think I might do to reduce the impact of this event?*

_____

_____

_____

_____

_____

**FIGURE 9.7    *Self-Assessment Exercise 19:***
***Preparing for High-Risk Situations***

Refer to the Life Events Prediction Questionnaire that you completed in Figure 9.5. Select *one* of the events that you rated as *highly likely to occur* and that you rated yourself to be *very confident* that you could deal with it. Write down a plan that describes exactly how you would deal with this situation. Although you have not rated this to be a problematic situation, this exercise will give you some practice in the process of specifying and developing plans in preparation for events.

* *One example of a life event that is highly likely to occur and that I feel very confident that I could deal with is:*

_____

_____

* *How could this come about (i.e., under what circumstances)?*

_____

_____

_____

_____

* *When is this most likely to occur?*

_____

_____

_____

* *Why? How do I know?*

_____

_____

_____

_____

*Continued*

**FIGURE 9.7** *Continued*

---

• *What can I do, if anything, to prevent this from happening?* (Draw up a list of possible steps to prevent the occurrence of the event.)

_____

_____

_____

_____

• *Has something like this ever happened before? (If yes: When? What happened? How did I cope with it?)*

_____

_____

_____

_____

• *What were the negative consequences?*

_____

_____

_____

_____

• *Were there any positive consequences?*

_____

_____

_____

_____

**FIGURE 9.7** *Continued*

---

• *If this does happen, what will be its effect on me on this occasion? How might I* think *in response to the event? How might I* feel *in response to the event?*

_____

_____

_____

_____

• *What do I think I might do to reduce the impact of this event?*

_____

_____

_____

_____

_____

**FIGURE 9.8** *Self-Assessment Exercise 20:*
*Preparing for High-Risk Situations*

---

Once again, refer to the Life Events Prediction Questionnaire that you completed in Figure 9.5. Select *one* of the events that you rated as *highly likely to occur* and that you rated yourself to be *not very confident* that you could deal with it. Develop a plan that you could follow in order to deal with this situation. You might find this exercise a bit more difficult. Reread the plan that you developed for the previous exercise. Use this as a model to help you with this exercise.

• *One example of a life event that is highly likely to occur and that I do not feel very confident that I could deal with is:*

_____

_____

*Continued*

**FIGURE 9.8** *Continued*

---

• *How could this come about (i.e., under what circumstances)?*

_____

_____

_____

_____

• *When is this most likely to occur?*

_____

_____

_____

_____

• *Why? How do I know?*

_____

_____

_____

_____

• *What can I do, if anything, to prevent this from happening?* (Draw up a list of possible steps to prevent the occurrence of the event.)

_____

_____

_____

_____

**FIGURE 9.8** *Continued*

- *Has something like this ever happened before? (If yes; When? What happened? How did I cope with it?)*

_____

_____

_____

_____

- *What were the negative consequences?*

_____

_____

_____

- *Were there any positive consequences?*

_____

_____

_____

_____

- *If this does happen, what will be its effect on me on this occasion? How might I think in response to the event? How might I feel in response to the event?*

_____

_____

_____

_____

*Continued*

**FIGURE 9.8** *Continued*

---

• *What do I think that I might do to reduce the impact of this event?*

_____

_____

_____

_____

_____


**FIGURE 9.9** *Self-Assessment Exercise 21:*
*Preparing for High-Risk Situations*

---

To complete this exercise you will need to refer to your responses to the Tinnitus Self-Efficacy Questionnaire (Figure 9.3). Check for any items that you rated as 40 or less. These situations represent tasks that you are not very confident that you can deal with. You will need to develop some plan to work on them further in order to build up your confidence ratings. Select one item that received a rating of 40 or less and write this in the first space below. Then begin to develop a plan about how you can deal with this by considering the questions posed below. You can apply this same process to any other items that you rated your confidence to be 40 or less.

• *One situation that I am not very confident that I can deal with is:*

Situation 1: _____

• *What might reduce my confidence in dealing with this situation?* (Consider your thoughts, feelings, and behaviors in response to the situation.)

_____

_____

_____

**FIGURE 9.9** *Continued*

• *What might increase my confidence in dealing with this situation?* (Consider your thoughts, feelings, and behaviors in response to the situation.)

_____

_____

_____

_____

• *How could I approach this situation differently?* (Consider your thoughts, feelings, and behaviors in response to the situation.)

_____

_____

_____

• *What other self-control strategies might I use to deal with this?* (Develop a specific plan.)

_____

_____

_____

_____

## *Conclusion*

Once you have worked through the examples in Figures 9.6 to 9.9, you will have developed some specific plans that will help you respond to some potential high-risk situations or life events. We recommend that you adopt the same approach to any other high-risk situation that you identified in Self-Assessment Exercise 16 (Figure 9.4). Write down your plans to provide you with a step-by-step guide should any of these situations arise in the future. Keeping a written record of your plans will mean that you can easily retrieve them if needed. For each situation that you listed in Figure 9.4, provide an account of what you actually might do should it occur. Specify what constructive thoughts you might think, how you might be feeling, and what specific self-control strategies you might use to effectively manage the situation. Be as specific as possible in drawing up your plan of action and try to incorporate the self-instructional and problem-solving strategies that we described in Chapter 8.

In the following chapter we will examine the ways that you might minimize the extent to which your tinnitus interferes with your daily lifestyle. We will also begin to look at the bigger picture and suggest some methods by which you might start to set some longer-term goals for the future.

# 10

## Reducing the Impact of Tinnitus on Your Daily Lifestyle

*Once I understood the way that I had allowed the tinnitus to dictate my life, I decided to take some action and to regain some control. I realized that I had let it determine what I did, and when I did it. I had gotten to the point where I wouldn't accept social invitations—I'd take the "wait and see" approach. By that, I mean that I'd check out how my tinnitus was on the day, and then decide whether to go to golf, or to a social function I'd been invited to, or whether I'd take the boat out as planned. It really got to the point where apart from work, I was not doing all that much! The less I did, the more time I had to focus on the noise in my head, and the more miserable I became!*

### Lifestyle and Tinnitus

In this section we will examine the ways in which lifestyle and tinnitus can be related. As we discussed in Chapter 1, a common problem associated with tinnitus is the extent to which it interferes with activities of daily living. Tinnitus might lead some people to reduce their involvement in pleasant and rewarding activities. Likewise, a low rate of involvement in activities may allow the tinnitus to assume a larger role in your life than would otherwise have been the case. One further goal is for you to take some steps to minimize the extent to which tinnitus interferes with your daily activities and to find ways to enjoy more activities.

## Increasing Pleasant Events

Pleasant events are activities that are intrinsically positive in their own right, providing an important source of pleasure, satisfaction, and enjoyment. A high level of participation in pleasant activities may also help reduce the aversiveness of unpleasant events, such as tinnitus. It might be the case that, apart from going to work or doing the things that you feel obliged to do (e.g., housework, washing, ironing), you do not spend much time simply doing things that you enjoy. Alternatively, you might be able to identify a few activities that you enjoy but that you don't do very often. In either case, it is important for you to spend some time trying to identify those activities that you enjoy and to begin to schedule these into your daily routine.

## Self-Assessment Exercise 22: Identifying Pleasant Events

In Figure 10.1 we present Self-Assessment Exercise 22 for you to complete. We have listed a range of activities that many people might find enjoyable. A few specific examples are provided, but the list is not exhaustive. When you read through these examples you will notice that some of the activities can be performed alone (e.g., reading a book); others can be performed with your partner or friends (e.g., playing tennis, entertaining friends). Some of the activities require some planning and cost (e.g., going to a restaurant or a concert); others are simple and cost nothing (e.g., sitting in the

**FIGURE 10.1  *Self Assessment Exercise 22: Identifying Pleasant Events***

Read through the activities and examples and then in the space provided write down some activities that you personally find enjoyable.

- Social activities (e.g., having a dinner party, going on a picnic with friends, having a barbecue with friends, going to a coffee shop with a friend, inviting a friend over for lunch, going to a social club, talking to a friend over the phone, chatting to a neighbor)

_____

_____

_____

_____

- Recreational activities (e.g., flying a kite, hiking/bushwalking, playing cards with friends, bowling, learning to dive, watching a football match, joining a choir, ballroom dancing)

_____

_____

_____

_____

- Sporting activities (e.g., playing golf, sailing, swimming, walking, playing tennis, surfing, going to the gym, jogging, doing yoga, attending aerobics classes, cycling, playing squash)

_____

_____

_____

_____

*Continued*

**FIGURE 10.1**  *Continued*

• Creative activities (e.g., writing poetry, doing pottery, painting, drawing, doing woodwork, building model airplanes, dressmaking, cooking, trying new recipes, making flower arrangements, gardening, doing craft work, renovating)

_____

_____

_____

_____

• Educational activities (e.g., learning a foreign language, going to a workshop or a class, taking a course on computers, history, politics, astronomy, etc., watching current affairs programs on TV, going to a public lecture)

_____

_____

_____

_____

• Solitary activities (e.g., reading a book, doing a crossword puzzle, sitting in the sun, listening to the radio, reading a magazine, practicing meditation, window-shopping, writing letters to friends, enjoying a quiet cup of coffee, relaxing in a warm bath)

_____

_____

_____

_____

• Artistic activities (e.g., visiting an art gallery, going to the opera, viewing a photo-graphic exhibition, going to the ballet, attending art appreciation classes, going to the theatre)

_____

**FIGURE 10.1** *Continued*

_____

_____

_____

- Pampering activities (e.g., having a massage, having a facial, going to the hair-dresser, having a pedicure, taking a warm bath, having a foot massage, sleeping in late, going to bed early)

_____

_____

_____

_____

- Musical activities (e.g., playing a musical instrument, learning to play a musical instrument, listening to favorite music, attending a concert, singing)

_____

_____

_____

_____

- Interest-oriented activities (e.g., collecting stamps or coins, going to fashion shows, visiting antique markets, doing photography, going to the races, reading skiing magazines, visiting historical sights such as old houses, churches)

_____

_____

_____

_____

*Continued*

**FIGURE 10.1**  *Continued*

---

- Travel activities (e.g., planning an overseas holiday, camping, country driving, weekend escapes, taking a "mystery" airplane flight, reading travel books, looking at photo albums from past holidays)

_____

_____

_____

_____

- Food activities (e.g., going to a favorite restaurant, entertaining friends, taking a cooking class, learning wine appreciation, reading recipe books, reading magazines on food and wine, exploring a new delicatessen, going to a food fair, going to a wine tasting, visiting Chinatown, trying a new cuisine, planning a menu for a dinner party, cooking, eating a slice of chocolate cake)

_____

_____

_____

_____

---

sun or singing). As you read through each of the various types of activities ask yourself the following questions:

- Do I enjoy doing this activity?
- If yes: What do I enjoy about it? When did I last do this? Would I like to do it more often? Why did I stop doing it? Who could I do it with?

Once you have completed the exercise in Figure 10.1, read through the example of potential pleasant events in Figure 10.2 and then record your own list of pleasant events in Figure 10.3.

**FIGURE 10.2** *Record of My Pleasant Events: Example*

| | |
|---|---|
| 1. | Having friends over for dinner |
| 2. | Having a facial |
| 3. | Working in the garden |
| 4. | Joining a bowling club |
| 5. | Learning to speak French |
| 6. | Going on holiday in Bordeaux |
| 7. | Relaxing in the sun |
| 8. | Reading a good novel |
| 9. | Sleeping in |
| 10. | Going for a walk along the beach |
| 11. | Writing letters to friends |
| 12. | Spending time with my partner |
| 13. | Trying a new recipe |
| 14. | Going to an art gallery |
| 15. | Watching the sunset |
| 16. | Shopping for new clothes |
| 17 | Going on a picnic with friends |
| 18. | Singing in a choir |
| 19. | Restoring antique furniture |
| 20. | Doing volunteer work |

**FIGURE 10.3**  *Record of My Pleasant Events: Exercise*

In the space below list all the activities that you have identified as potential pleasant events.

| | |
|---|---|
| 1. | |
| 2. | |
| 3. | |
| 4. | |
| 5. | |
| 6. | |
| 7. | |
| 8. | |
| 9. | |
| 10. | |
| 11. | |
| 12. | |
| 13. | |
| 14. | |
| 15. | |
| 16. | |
| 17 | |
| 18. | |
| 19. | |
| 20. | |

## Scheduling Pleasant Events

Now that you have identified a list of activities that you find enjoyable, the next step is to begin to schedule pleasant activities into each week. We will refer to this as *activity scheduling*. The aim of activity scheduling is for you to gradually increase the range and frequency of pleasant activities that you participate in. To begin, select three to four activities from your list of pleasant events and write these in the Record of Weekly Pleasant Activities recording form, which is provided in Figure 10.4. In Figure 10.5 we provide an

**FIGURE 10.4** *Record of Weekly Pleasant Activities*

| | **Days** | | | | | | |
|---|---|---|---|---|---|---|---|
| | 1 | 2 | 3 | 4 | 5 | 6 | 7 |
| | ___day | ___ day | ___ day | ___ day | ___ day | ___ day | ___ day |

*Activities*

1. _____

2. _____

3. _____

4. _____

5. _____

6. _____

7. _____

8. _____

9. _____

10. _____

*Source:* Henry & Wilson, 2001

**FIGURE 10.5**   *Example of Record of Weekly Pleasant Activities*

| Day | 1 Tuesday | 2 Wednesday | 3 Thursday | 4 Friday | 5 Saturday | 6 Sunday | 7 Monday |
|---|---|---|---|---|---|---|---|
| *Activities* | | | | | | | |
| 1. Listen to radio | X | X | X | X | X | | |
| 2. Go and see a movie | | | | | | X | |
| 3. Lunch for John & Ann | | | | | | | X |
| 4. Read a magazine | | | | | X | | |
| 5. Relax in a warm bath | | | X | | | | X |

example to illustrate how you might complete this form. It is important that you plan to do a certain number of pleasant activities each week. Even the actual planning of events can itself be intrinsically pleasant. For example, imagine how enjoyable it can be simply anticipating going to your favorite restaurant at the end of the week. At the beginning of each week plan your weekly pleasant events. Set yourself a specific goal (e.g., you plan to participate in five pleasant activities over the coming week). At the end of the week check your recording sheet to see whether you achieved your goal. If so, remember to praise yourself for your efforts.

## *Gradual Introduction of Pleasant Events*

Some pleasant activities may take a great deal more time to organize than others. For example, if your goal is to go hiking, you would need to do quite a deal of preparation. You can introduce these events by a graded approach in which you break down the overall plan into small, manageable steps. The steps in going hiking could be (1) checking the telephone book, or local paper for details of hiking clubs; (2) contacting a hiking club; (3) finding out about forthcoming club outings; (4) selecting a specific walk that interests you; (5) getting out your walking shoes; (6) drawing up a list of items that you need for the outing (maps, food, camping equipment, etc.); and

(7) buying and assembling together all the items. These steps could be scheduled so that you finally reach the point when you can join the group to go on a hike. The point here is that such an outing will not take place unless you make a start on the arrangements. You also might consider: What are the possible obstacles to completing this goal? How can these obstacles be overcome? You might even apply the problem-solving strategies to find a solution to these potential obstacles.

If you wanted to go to a play or concert, the list might look like the following: (1) contacting the relevant organizers in order to get the schedule of forthcoming performances; (2) contacting a friend who may wish to go with you; (3) discussing with the friend the options for performances and dates; (4) buying the tickets; (5) planning the event: Will you wish to have a meal? If so, what restaurant will you go to? How will you travel to the theatre?

If any of your proposed pleasant events are of a similar degree of complexity, you might make a list of the steps that will be required in order to reach the final goal.

## Self-Assessment Exercise 23: Lifestyle Modifications

Another goal that you can begin to work on as you start to make progress relates to broader areas of your life: Are there any longer-term changes that you might wish to make to your life that would assist you in having a more enjoyable time? Are there broad goals that you have hoped to reach concerning work, education, or recreation? It might be useful to ask yourself the question: *Are there ways in which my life can be improved—even in small ways?* Take a moment to consider various aspects of your lifestyle. To help you in this process, complete Self-Assessment Exercise 23 provided in Figure 10.6. In Figure 10.7 we provide an example of a plan for making some changes to specific aspects of your life.

**FIGURE 10.6** *Self-Assessment Exercise 23:*
*Making Lifestyle Changes*

Listed below are some broad areas that contribute to a person's lifestyle. Consider each individual area to determine whether there are any things that you would like to change within each area (i.e., something you would like to do more often or less often). Should you identify any specific areas that you are dissatisfied with, these can be worked on in the longer term.

**My Current Work**

- *Am I satisfied with this area of my life?*

_____

_____

- *Can I be specific about what I want to change?*

_____

_____

- *Where would I like to be in 5 years' time? Or even 2 years?*

_____

_____

- *How can I get there?*

_____

_____

- *What do I need to do now so that my goals can be reached?* (Develop a plan and be as specific as possible.)

_____

_____

**FIGURE 10.6** *Continued*

**My Work-Related Goals and Ambitions**

- *Am I satisfied with this area of my life?*

_____

_____

- *Can I be specific about what I want to change?*

_____

_____

- *Where would I like to be in 5 years' time? Or even 2 years?*

_____

_____

- *How can I get there?*

_____

_____

- *What do I need to do now so that my goals can be reached?* (Develop a plan and be as specific as possible.)

_____

_____

**My Relationship with My Spouse/Partner**

- *Am I satisfied with this area of my life?*

_____

_____

*Continued*

**FIGURE 10.6** *Continued*

---

- *Can I be specific about what I want to change?*

  _____

  _____

- *Where would I like to be in 5 years' time? Or even 2 years?*

  _____

  _____

- *How can I get there?*

  _____

  _____

- *What do I need to do now so that my goals can be reached?* (Develop a plan and be as specific as possible.)

  _____

  _____

**My Relationship with My Children, Parents, or Other Important Family Members**

- *Am I satisfied with this area of my life?*

  _____

  _____

- *Can I be specific about what I want to change?*

  _____

  _____

- *Where would I like to be in 5 years' time? Or even 2 years?*

  _____

  _____

**FIGURE 10.6** *Continued*

• *How can I get there?*

_____

_____

• *What do I need to do now so that my goals can be reached?* (Develop a plan and be as specific as possible.)

_____

_____

**My Social Relationships Outside the Family**

• *Am I satisfied with this area of my life?*

_____

_____

• *Can I be specific about what I want to change?*

_____

_____

• *Where would I like to be in 5 years' time? Or even 2 years?*

_____

_____

• *How can I get there?*

_____

_____

*Continued*

**FIGURE 10.6** *Continued*

- *What do I need to do now so that my goals can be reached?* (Develop a plan and be as specific as possible.)

_____

_____

**My Financial and Housing Situation**

- *Am I satisfied with this area of my life?*

_____

_____

- *Can I be specific about what I want to change?*

_____

_____

- *Where would I like to be in 5 years' time? Or even 2 years?*

_____

_____

- *How can I get there?*

_____

_____

- *What do I need to do now so that my goals can be reached?* (Develop a plan and be as specific as possible.)

_____

_____

**FIGURE 10.6** *Continued*

**My Educational Pursuits**

- *Am I satisfied with this area of my life?*

_____

_____

- *Can I be specific about what I want to change?*

_____

_____

- *Where would I like to be in 5 years' time? Or even 2 years?*

_____

_____

- *How can I get there?*

_____

_____

- *What do I need to do now so that my goals can be reached?* (Develop a plan and be as specific as possible.)

_____

_____

**My General Goals in Life**

- *Am I satisfied with this area of my life?*

_____

_____

*Continued*

**FIGURE 10.6**  *Continued*

---

- *Can I be specific about what I want to change?*

  _____

  _____

- *Where would I like to be in 5 years' time? Or even 2 years?*

  _____

  _____

- *How can I get there?*

  _____

  _____

- *What do I need to do now so that my goals can be reached? (Develop a plan and be as specific as possible.)*

  _____

  _____

---

**FIGURE 10.7**  *An Example of a Plan for Making Lifestyle Modifications*

---

Identified area of dissatisfaction = I am not satisfied with my current work situation.

- *Am I satisfied with this area of my life?*
  No. I have become stuck in a rut. I have been at this job for eight years.
  I know I could do so much more, but there is no potential for advancement in this job.

- *Can I be specific about what I want to change?*
  I need a job that is more challenging and where I can really reach my potential.

**FIGURE 10.7** *Continued*

---

- *Where would I like to be in 5 years' time? Or even 2 years?*
  *In two years time I would like to be in a senior position in a company.*

- *How can I get there?*
  *I need to make the decision to start looking for another job. I also need to take a few courses to update my management and computer skills.*

- *What do I need to do now so that my goals can be reached?* (Develop a plan and be as specific as possible.)
  *The first step is probably to update my resume. I might go to an employment agency to get some tips on how best to present this. I'll make contact with a few people to ask them if they'll provide references for me. Then I need to begin to check the employment section of the paper. I'll phone the local college and ask them to send me some information on their business and management courses. I'll decide on which course is best and put an application in.*

---

## Conclusion

This chapter has been concerned with the connection between tinnitus and your general lifestyle, including participation in enjoyable activities and making progress toward specific longer-term life goals. The aim of this chapter was to help you to see that management of your tinnitus involves balancing various aspects of your life. One person who attended one of our group programs commented in an early session that their world was "full of tinnitus—there is nothing but the tinnitus." It is easy to imagine how this state of affairs may come about. In order for your world to not be described in this way, you need to be able to allocate time to other important activities and goals. Participation in your own, self-defined pleasant activities is one way to allocate a place to tinnitus and a place to important sources of enjoyment. If you are involved in a range of rewarding activities, including hobbies, pastimes, educational pursuits—whatever brings you pleasure—you will not only have a better time but you will also reduce your risk of depression, increase your satisfaction with life, and gain greater control over your tinnitus. If tinnitus gets you down and prevents you from doing the things that you enjoy, these problems can provide a warning signal that you need to take control over the tinnitus—put it in its place in your life.

# 11

## *Maintaining Gains in the Longer Term*

*After I attended the group I realized that I could learn some ways to control my tinnitus. Actually, I noticed that for years I have been using some similar strategies to deal with pressures and demands at work. I never thought to try to apply these same techniques to my tinnitus. It has not been easy, I have to admit, but I tried to view it as a challenge. I started to think, "Blasted noise, I've had you getting in the way of things; so things are going to change." It's taken some time and a lot of effort. Some days are still a bit more of a challenge than others. But that's life, isn't it? On the whole, I can say I'm getting on top of it. I really don't notice it as much.*

### *Maintaining Gains*

In this chapter we will discuss methods that you can use to maintain the gains and progress you have made so far. The aim of this part of your self-management program is to help you acquire better skills for the long-term management of your tinnitus. All of the self-control strategies described in this book require consistent and regular practice in order to develop skill in applying each of the specific techniques. As your skill increases, and once you are able to successfully employ the various techniques to manage your tinnitus, it is likely that you will begin to use them fairly automatically. This, in turn, will give rise to a shift in your cognitive, perceptual, emotional, and behavioral responses to your tinnitus. As you change the way that you react to tinnitus, you will probably find it to be less problematic, and in time, you will simply not notice the tinnitus as often.

Why might you need to acquire better skills for the long-term management of your tinnitus? *Chronic tinnitus,* by definition, is an audiological problem whereby a person needs to adapt to a continuous negative sensation. Furthermore, as we discussed in Chapter 1, tinnitus is often accompanied by a number of emotional difficulties (e.g., anxiety, depression, anger), sleep problems, and disruptions to occupational, leisure, and social activities. You can learn to adapt to tinnitus and to change the way that you respond to the sensation via alterations in your perceptual, cognitive, and emotional processes. However, not only do you need to learn methods of managing tinnitus in the short term (i.e., under present life circumstances) but you also need to be able to acquire longer-term strategies so that you can deal with potential changes in your life circumstances. These changed life circumstances might include alterations in your emotional state, the presence of adverse life events, and periodic changes in the audiological aspects of your tinnitus or other hearing problems.

## What Factors Might Interfere with Effective Management of Tinnitus?

There are a number of factors that might interfere with your ability to manage tinnitus in the longer-term. These sources of interference might include:

1. Failure to use, or infrequent use of, self-control strategies
2. Increased symptoms of emotional distress, such as depression, tension, irritability, anger, and sleep problems (possibly not caused by the tinnitus)

3. Negative life events (not caused by tinnitus), such as bereavement or loss of job
4. Negative life events related to tinnitus, such as loss of job or marital conflict
5. Maladaptive behaviors, such as ceasing or decreasing participation in recreational or occupational activities
6. Tinnitus/hearing-related effects, such as difficulties hearing conversations in noisy places as well as difficulties in quiet places
7. Social or interpersonal aspects, such as lack of understanding from spouse, family, or friends

If you find that you are going through a period of increasing difficulty with your tinnitus, you may need to consider which of the preceding issues may be the cause of interference with your progress. It is only when you have correctly analyzed the cause of the difficulties that you can develop a plan to improve the situation. As part of this self-management approach, you need to be able to take stock of the situation on a regular basis. The following exercises can help you by providing a regular evaluation of your progress.

## *Self-Assessment Exercises 24 and 25: Assessing Your Progress*

In order to assess your progress we suggest that you take some time each month to review how you are managing your tinnitus. To assist you in this process we provide an example of a recording form in Figure 11.1. In this example, the time line shows how a person has managed his tinnitus in the previous four weeks.

We have provided a blank recording form in Figure 11.2 for you to monitor the general pattern of your emotional well-being over a four-week period.

**FIGURE 11.1**  *Self-Assessment Exercise 24: Review of Past Four Weeks (Example)*

This form is designed to help you track how things have been going in the past four weeks. The idea is to draw a line that describes the changes in the way in which tinnitus has affected your feelings and well-being over the past four weeks. The example shown here may serve as a guide to the way in which the plot can be drawn.

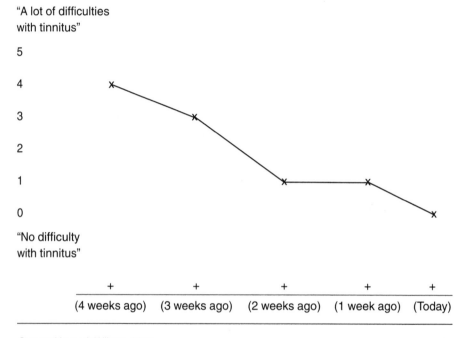

"A lot of difficulties
with tinnitus"

"No difficulty
with tinnitus"

*Source:* Henry & Wilson, 2001

The main purpose of your monthly reviews is to consider your progress with your self-management program. That is, to what extent have you been practicing and applying your self-control strategies to manage any tinnitus-related problems, or any other stressful events that you might have encountered? To assist you in

**FIGURE 11.2** *Self-Assessment Exercise 24: Review of Past Four Weeks*

This form is designed to help you track how things have been going in the past four weeks. The idea is to draw a line that describes the changes in the way in which tinnitus has affected your feelings and well-being over the past four weeks.

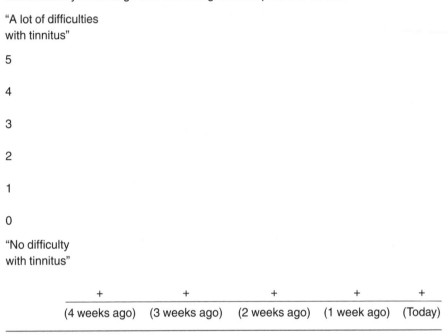

"A lot of difficulties
with tinnitus"

5

4

3

2

1

0

"No difficulty
with tinnitus"

| + | + | + | + | + |
|---|---|---|---|---|
| (4 weeks ago) | (3 weeks ago) | (2 weeks ago) | (1 week ago) | (Today) |

*Source:* Henry & Wilson, 2001

this process, Self-Assessment Exercise 25, described in Figure 11.3, provides you with a progress and maintenance checklist for you to complete. You might also want to reread the material in Chapter 3 and complete some of the daily diary records and questionnaires provided in that chapter.

**FIGURE 11.3** *Self-Assessment Exercise 25:*
*Progress and Maintenance Checklist*

Listed below are the primary self-control techniques that we have introduced you to in this book. Use this checklist in order to assess your progress and maintenance in the application of these techniques.

1. Acknowledging the connection between thoughts and emotions (review Chapter 4)
   - *Have I been using the A-B-C model?*
   - *Have I been aware of the impact of situations on my emotions?*
   - *Have I noticed changes in my mood and tried to identify possible causes?*

2. Recognizing negative automatic thoughts (review Chapter 4)
   - *Have I been using the A-B-C model to monitor my thoughts?*
   - *Have I been aware of the presence of negative automatic thoughts?*

3. Challenging negative automatic thoughts (review Chapter 5)
   - *Have I been applying the A-B-C-D-E model?*
   - *Have I been using my thought-stopping techniques as a means of hitting the "pause" button to interrupt the flow of negative thoughts?*
   - *Have I been using my distraction techniques to allow some "time-out"?*
   - *Have I been challenging any negative thoughts and then substituting them with more constructive thoughts?*
   - *Have I been applying the A-B-C-D-E model to deal with any distressing emotions?*
   - *Have I been able to generate some positive thoughts about myself?*
   - *Have I been using some regular cue as a reminder to generate some positive thoughts about myself and my present life circumstances?*

4. Recognizing levels of physical tension and signs of stress (review Chapter 6)
   - *Have I been practicing my relaxation techniques?*
   - *Have I been tuning into my tension zones during each day?*
   - *Have I been applying my relaxation techniques during my daily routine to control any increases in my tension levels?*
   - *Have I been using my relaxation techniques to deal with any sleep problems?*
   - *Have I been using my relaxation techniques to deal with quiet situations?*
   - *Have I been using my relaxation techniques to deal with noisy situations?*
   - *Have I been using my relaxation techniques to deal with stressful situations?*
   - *Have I been using my relaxation techniques to help me to concentrate on any demanding mental tasks?*

5. Recognizing times when tinnitus is the focus of my attention (review Chapter 7)
   - *Have I been practicing my attention control techniques?*

**FIGURE 11.3** *Continued*

- *Have I been applying my attention control techniques whenever my tinnitus becomes the focus of my attention?*
- *Have I been practicing my imagery skills?*
- *Have I been using my imagery skills to reduce focusing my attention on tinnitus?*
- *Have I been using my imagery techniques to try to alter my tinnitus in some way?*
- *Have I been using my attention control and/or imagery skills to assist me to deal with quiet times?*
- *Have I been using my attention control and/or imagery skills to assist me to deal with noisy times?*
- *Have I been using my attention control and/or imagery skills to assist me to deal with any sleep problems?*
- *Have I been using my attention control and/or imagery skills to assist me in concentrating on some mental task?*

6. Integrating my self-control strategies (review Chapter 8)
   - *Have I been using self-instructions to deal with stressful situations?*
   - *Have I been using self-instructions as a reminder to use all of my self-control strategies?*
   - *Have I been using the presence of negative thoughts as a cue to use self-instructions?*
   - *Have I been using self-instructions to anticipate what I want to do in order to deal with stressful situations?*
   - *Have I been using self-instructions to plan how to deal with stressful situations?*
   - *Have I been using problem-solving skills to deal with difficult daily situations?*
   - *Have I been using problem-solving skills to deal with difficult tinnitus-related situations?*

7. Dealing with high-risk situations (review Chapter 9)
   - *Have I identified high-risk situations that are relevant to me?*
   - *Have I developed some specific plans for dealing with each of these situations?*
   - *Have I used any of my plans to prepare for and deal with any high-risk situations that might have arisen?*
   - *Have I developed some specific plans for dealing with those situations that I still do not feel very confident that I could deal with? Have I implemented any of these plans to help me to build my confidence in dealing with these specific situations?*
   - *Have I developed some specific plans for dealing with potential problematic situations that might arise in the future? Have I used any of my plans to prepare*

*Continued*

**FIGURE 11.3** *Continued*

---

*for and deal with any of these problematic situations that might have arisen in the past month?*

8. Reducing the extent to which tinnitus interferes with my daily lifestyle (review Chapter 10)
   - *Have I identified the ways in which tinnitus interferes with my daily lifestyle?*
   - *Have I identified some pleasant activities?*
   - *Have I been scheduling some pleasant activities into my daily routine?*
   - *Have I been setting some goals to ensure that each week I participate in pleasant events?*
   - *Have I been rewarding myself for scheduling some pleasant activities?*
   - *Have I considered my lifestyle in the longer term to determine if I wish to make any modifications to my life?*
   - *Have I made any goals to make longer-term lifestyle modifications? What progress am I making in reaching my goals?*

---

## Conclusion

In this chapter we have outlined the steps that you might take to ensure that you can maintain your progress over a long period of time. Your ability to manage the tinnitus may be challenged from time to time by other events in your life or by changes in the tinnitus itself. If you become aware of any decrease in your ability to manage your tinnitus, it is best to use this occasion as a signal that it is time to invest more of your attention on dealing with the problem. Remember that the aim is for you to take control over the tinnitus, not for the tinnitus to take control over you. Perhaps you could reread sections of this book in times of difficulty in order to remind yourself about the ways in which you can manage the tinnitus. We also hope that many of you will not really need this chapter—but it is included just in case you need extra help from time to time!

# 12

# *Some Final Tips on Managing Your Tinnitus*

In Chapter 1 we began by discussing some of the common problems that people might experience in relation to tinnitus. These problems are summarized in Figure 12.1. In this chapter we will offer you some further tips on how to manage some of these common problems.

## *Dealing with Distressing Emotions*

In order to manage the distressing emotional problems that might arise in response to tinnitus, it is important for you to keep in mind the powerful influence of your thoughts on your emotions. You can learn to reduce feelings of depression, low mood, helplessness, and hopelessness by practicing the cognitive methods that are described in Chapters 4 and 5. Symptoms of anxiety, tension, and frustration may also be addressed by these cognitive strategies in combination with the relaxation procedures described in Chapter 6. Relaxation training will also assist you if you find that your tinnitus is worse when you are under some form of stress. The self-instructional and

**FIGURE 12.1** *Summary of Common Problems Associated with Tinnitus*

---

1. *Distressing Emotional Problems*
   • Tinnitus causes feelings of depression, tension, irritability, anger, annoyance, and frustration.
   • Tinnitus is worse during periods of stress.

2. *Sleep Difficulties*
   • Tinnitus causes problems in falling asleep.
   • Tinnitus makes it difficult to remain asleep.

3. *Detrimental Effects on Hearing and Communication*
   • Tinnitus makes it difficult to follow conversations or to hear what is being said against background noise.
   • Tinnitus causes problems in quiet environments.
   • Tinnitus causes problems in noisy places.

4. *Intrusiveness on Daily Activities and Lifestyle*
   • Tinnitus disrupts one's ability to concentrate on work activities and other mental tasks.
   • Tinnitus causes negative changes in relationships with spouse, partner, family members, and friends.
   • Tinnitus leads to reduced participation in work, social, and recreational activities.
   • Tinnitus leads to reduced pleasure from social, leisure, and recreational activities.

---

problem-solving skills described in Chapter 8, and the procedures for identifying and preparing for high-risk situations, can also all serve as effective methods to manage stressful events. Feelings of helplessness and frustration may be overcome by learning to gain a greater sense of control over your attentional processes in response to tinnitus using the attention control and imagery exercises described in Chapter 7. We will now spend some time offering a few further tips on how to deal with feelings of suicide and anger.

## Suicide

In Chapter 3 we provided some guidance for self-assessment of tinnitus. In that section of the book, and in other places, we have mentioned the fact that some people with tinnitus contemplate committing suicide. We may consider at this point in the book three different types of experiences that may arise in relation to suicide. Some people are aware of suicidal thoughts, but are confident that they will not actually carry through with any suicidal actions. Others are troubled by suicidal thoughts, even to the point of making plans. On occasion, such people may get to the brink of suicide. A third group of people may make an attempt to kill themselves, but, for various reasons, do not succeed. Even if a person does not intend to carry out a suicidal plan, the thoughts themselves can be very frightening.

Clearly, this book is not intended to be a substitute for professional assistance for any person who thinks about suicide. These thoughts or plans should serve as a signal that *appropriate professional assistance ought to be sought*. It is imperative that you mention these issues to your regular medical practitioner, specialist, or other member of the helping professions with whom you are in contact. That person can then consider whether you would benefit from a referral to a clinical psychologist or psychiatrist. Of course, you may realize that your situation is desperate and that more rapid action is needed. If so, you may decide to refer yourself for an appropriate consultation. (We are aware that different referral practices occur in different parts of the world.) The important point here is not to panic, nor to give up. You must not give up the hope of finding help—help is available. Professional assistance may be needed to find that help. By all means, take this book with you, because you may be able to use relevant sections of this book to highlight the most urgent issues for you.

## Anger

Some people who experience tinnitus display a great deal of anger. This display of anger often consumes an unnecessary amount of energy that could be better harnessed in directly dealing with the problems. In addition, anger tends to be very difficult for other people, such as friends and family, to cope with.

If anger is a problem, you need to think about how to manage it while still expressing your legitimate frustrations in other more productive ways. It is more effective to be assertive in a way that respects the rights and feelings of other people.

Ask yourself: What or who is the real subject of this anger? Sometimes the anger is just being directed at anyone, even when these people are not the real or legitimate object of the frustration. The common objects of anger are the person, company, or institution that might be responsible for causing the tinnitus; other people who do not display an adequate understanding of the tinnitus, and who therefore do not provide the support that is expected; people who make loud noises or are responsible for noisy machinery; the medical profession for failing to provide a cure; or the government for not spending more money on tinnitus research.

Of course, a person who experiences tinnitus may be angry about various issues that have no relevance to the tinnitus, although tinnitus may increase the frustration level, making it difficult to deal with annoying events in a calmer, more accepting way. If you can identify who (or what) it is that makes you angry, you may then be able to develop a plan to deal with the problem more appropriately. You could tackle this issue as a subject of the problem-solving exercises that were described in Chapter 8. You need to identify the thoughts that connect the events with the emotion of anger using the A-B-C analysis, as described in Chapter 4. Having identified the thoughts, and examined their validity or constructiveness, you can then generate more constructive and appropriate counter-statements. The applied relaxation techniques described in Chapter 6 might also be used to deal with specific events that make you angry, even if these events are unrelated to the tinnitus.

## Sleep Difficulties

If you experience any problems with sleep, there are a number of techniques described in this book on which you might wish to focus. In particular, we recommend that you use the relaxation techniques described in Chapter 6. Learning effective relaxation skills will help you achieve deep levels of physical relaxation. A reduction in physical tension will produce a physical state that is conducive for sleep. Relaxation can help decrease the time it takes to fall asleep as well as improve the quality of your sleep.

If you find that you are troubled by any worrying or racing thoughts when you are trying to get to sleep, the cognitive strategies described in Chapters 4 and 5 might prove to be very useful. For example, you might notice specific thoughts running through your mind, such as "I won't be able to function at work tomorrow," "I can't cope without sleep," "I'll never get back to sleep," "This is awful." Clearly, these thoughts could be subjected to the cognitive restructuring methods described in Chapter 5, and more constructive thoughts might be substituted in their place. In addition to this suggestion, it might be very useful to use some of the thought-stopping and distraction exercises contained in Chapter 5. For instance, you might try imagining a large flashing stop sign and then participate in a distraction exercise, such as counting backwards by 7s from 300 or going through the alphabet backwards. You could combine these mental tasks with some relaxation procedure. That is, as you count or recite the alphabet, with each number or letter that comes to mind, deliberately focus on releasing any physical tension from your body.

One thing that it is important to avoid is simply lying in bed, tossing and turning! If you have not been able to fall asleep within about 20 minutes, get out of bed and go into another room. You might then try focusing on some relaxing activity, such as reading a book, thumbing through a magazine, or watching television. Whatever task you choose, be sure that it is not overly stimulating or too exciting. Only return to bed when you begin to feel sleepy.

In overcoming sleep problems it might also be useful to look more closely at how you spend your time from early evening to just prior to going to bed, and also the activities that you participate in while in your bedroom. To ensure that you maximize your quality of sleep, here is a list of things you might wish to consider:

- Your bed and bedroom should be reserved for the purposes of sleep and being intimate with your spouse or partner. Avoid other activities, such as completing tasks for work, working on your computer, reading or watching television, and so on.

- Keep to a regular time schedule. Go to bed at the same time each night and get out of bed at the same time each morning.
- Avoid taking any troubles or worries to bed with you. If necessary, spend some time in the early evening reflecting on your day and preparing for the next day.
- Regular exercise can improve your sleep. However, it is a good idea to restrict any vigorous exercise to the early evening (i.e., not immediately before bedtime).
- Spend a couple of hours prior to going to bed participating in some relaxing activities. Practice your relaxation training, take a warm bath or shower, have a warm milk drink, watch some relaxing television, listen to some soothing music, or read a book to unwind.
- Avoid alcoholic beverages in the time just prior to bed.
- Avoid going to bed hungry, as this is likely to disturb your sleep.
- Avoid taking any naps during the day.
- Reduce your caffeine intake throughout the day and particularly in the evening. Caffeine is a stimulant and is found in coffee, tea, and cola beverages.

## Coping with Noisy Situations

People with tinnitus often say that they do not like going into noisy situations. Clearly, avoidance of extremely noisy environments is good practice for everybody, but sometimes this avoidance can be taken to extremes. Some people even wear ear-protection devices in a wide variety of situations without any real need to do so. Many of these people have an extreme fear that the noise will damage their hearing or that the noise may create a burst of very loud tinnitus. Other people do not have any particular fear of the noise, but simply want to avoid any temporary increase in the loudness of the tinnitus, or they may find that it is very difficult to hear other people speaking in such noisy places. An increase in the loudness of the tinnitus may be noticed when the person moves from a noisy place to a quieter place.

Problems such as these may lead the person to stop going to events, such as parties, restaurants, musical concerts, movies, and the like. It is difficult to avoid noisy situations completely, and extreme avoidance may result in a reduction in participation in enjoyable activities. The negative effect of reducing enjoyable activities may result in a reduced quality of life.

If you are very sensitive to loud noises, a condition called *hyperacusis,* we suggest that you discuss this matter with your hearing specialist or audiologist. There may be some specific approaches that can be undertaken to assist you. Apart from hyperacusis, you may obtain some benefit from the attention control procedures or relaxation techniques (see Chapters 6 and 7). You could practice these techniques in slightly more noisy situations at home, under your own control. You might place some piece of equipment that makes a noise in the room while you practice the attention control and relaxation skills (e.g., bedside masker, noise generators, AM radio mistuned so as to get only static). You could then raise the volume a little higher each time you practice the techniques (or move the equipment closer to you over time). The equipment may be located in another room at first, but then you could move it into the room, and bring it closer over a period of weeks. We are not suggesting that you allow the noise level to be too extreme (that would be dangerous)—just allow the volume to occur at a slightly uncomfortable level, but one that would be tolerable to most people. The next step might involve imagining being in a range of natural noisy situations. When you feel comfortable with your progress, you might try to use the techniques in loud natural situations, such as at a shopping center or restaurant.

## Coping with Quiet Situations

In contrast to the difficulty with noisy situations, some people avoid quiet places because these situations make the tinnitus seem more intrusive and reminds them that they have lost the pleasure of "silence." This loss is experienced quite acutely by some people. Thus, participation in pleasant activities that normally take place in quiet areas may be less enjoyable because of the tinnitus. The attention control and imagery training techniques described in Chapters 6 and 7 may be of particular assistance to people with this kind of difficulty. You can begin by identifying the quiet situations that you either avoid or would prefer to avoid.

Return to the chapter on attentional control and imagery training (Chapter 7). You might practice these techniques in a succession of quieter situations at home. Perhaps place some piece of equipment that makes a noise in the room while you practice the attention control and relaxation skills, and then lower the volume a little further each time you practice the techniques. The next step might involve imagining being in a range of quiet situations, choosing some situations that are intrinsically very pleasant. When you feel comfortable with your progress, you might try to use the techniques in real-life quiet situations.

## *Impact on Daily Activities and Lifestyle*

The potential impact of tinnitus on your daily activities and lifestyle may be overcome by using strategies to increase your participation in pleasant activities and making modifications to certain areas of your lifestyle, such as those described in Chapter 10. Feelings of frustration and interpersonal problems might also arise because you feel that other people (e.g., your spouse, partner, friends, or family members) cannot appreciate what it is like to experience tinnitus. If this is the case, it might be very useful to suggest that other significant people in your life read this book. The contents of this book might help the people in your life to gain a greater understanding of some of the problems that you might be experiencing.

In this chapter we have identified several specific areas of concern to some people who experience tinnitus, and have provided further suggestions about dealing with these issues. For some of these problems, we suggest that you obtain more specialist assistance.

For other problems, such as dealing with loud or quiet situations, the suggestions provided here may help you overcome the problem. You might also consider making contact with one of the tinnitus self-help associations that exist in many parts of the world. These associations are listed in the Appendix at the end of this book.

## *General Conclusion*

We realize that there are quite a number of different ways in which tinnitus affects people. In this book we have provided numerous suggestions about the ways in which these problems can be overcome. As you can see, learning to live with the tinnitus is possible if you take control of the tinnitus instead of letting the tinnitus take control of you. We have described a large number of approaches to help you take control.

Our clinical experience has taught us that people vary widely in their reactions to the different approaches. Some people respond very well to some ideas, such as the relaxation training or the attention control techniques, and other people find the thought management (cognitive) strategies to be very useful. On numerous occasions we have found that people will react very positively to one seemingly simple suggestion, taking a single idea that then makes a real difference to their lives.

Perhaps you have read this book from cover to cover and have gained the general impression that you can do something but you are not sure exactly what to do now! We suggest that you reread the book over a period of several weeks, taking time to do the exercises in a systematic fashion. Try to experiment with all the ideas in the book, even the ones that you feel are less likely to be helpful, and actually give the ideas a trial period. You could keep track of your progress by using the forms supplied in Chapter 3. It may be helpful to know that many of the ideas contained in the book have been developed with people, just like you, who experience tinnitus. We are indebted to the many individuals who have shared their experiences of tinnitus with us over the years. Like many of those people, we hope that you also find the suggestions made in this book to be valuable in allowing you to live a fulfilling life, despite your tinnitus. As one person in our group commented, *"I now think of the tinnitus as part of me, and that's O.K.—I know how I can take control!"*

# Additional Reading

Andersson, G., Melin, L., Hagnebo, C., Scott, B., & Lindberg, P. (1995). A review of psychological treatment approaches for patients suffering from tinnitus. *Annals of Behavioural Medicine, 17*, 357–366.

Aug, J., Kavanagh, D., & Wilson, P. H. (1987). *Tinnitus self-efficacy questionnaire.* Unpublished test.

Bakal, D. (1982). *The psychobiology of chronic headache.* New York: Springer.

Beck, A. T., Rush, A. J., Shaw, B. F., & Emery, G. (1979). *Cognitive therapy for depression.* New York: Guilford Press.

Bernstein, D. A., & Borkovec, T. D. (1973). *Progressive relaxation training: A manual for the helping professions.* Champaign, IL: Research Press.

Davies, S., McKenna, L., & Hallam, R. S. (1995). Relaxation and cognitive therapy: A controlled trial in chronic tinnitus. *Psychology and Health, 10*, 129–143.

Goebel, G., Hiller, W., Fruhauf, K., & Fichter, M. M. (1992). Effects of inpatient multimodal behavioural treatment on complex chronic tinnitus. In J-M Aran & R. Dauman (Eds.), *Tinnitus 91. Proceedings of the Fourth International Tinnitus Seminar* (pp. 465–470). Amsterdam: Kugler Publications.

Hallam, R. S., Rachman, S., & Hinchcliffe, R. (1984). Psychological aspects of tinnitus. In S. Rachman (Ed.), *Contributions to medical psychology* (vol. 3). Oxford: Pergamon Press.

Henry, J. L., & Wilson, P. (1996). The psychological management of tinnitus: Comparison of a combined cognitive educational program, education alone and a waiting-list control. *International Tinnitus Journal, 2*, 9–20.

Henry, J. L., & Wilson, P. H. (2001). *The psychological management of chronic tinnitus: A cognitive-behavioral approach.* Boston: Allyn and Bacon.

Jakes, S. C., Hallam, R. S., McKenna, L., & Hinchcliffe, R. (1992). Group cognitive therapy for medical patients: An application to tinnitus. *Cognitive Therapy and Research, 16,* 67–82.

Jakubowski, P., & Lange, A. J. (1978). *The assertive option: Your rights and responsibilities.* Champaign, IL: Research Press.

Kanfer, F. H., & Goldstein, A. P. (Eds.). (1975). *Helping people change: A textbook of methods.* New York: Pergamon Press.

Kavanagh, D. J., & Wilson, P. H. (1987). Prediction of outcome with group cognitive therapy for depression. *Behaviour Research and Therapy, 27,* 333–343.

Lewinsohn, P. M., Munoz, R. F., Youngren, M. A., & Zeiss, A. M. (1978). *Control your depression.* Englewood Cliffs, NJ: Prentice-Hall.

Lindberg, P., Scott, B., Melin, L., & Lyttkens, L. (1987). Long-term effects of psychological treatment of tinnitus. *Scandinavian Audiology, 16,* 2–5.

Lindberg, P., Scott, B., Melin, L., & Lyttkens, L. (1988). Behavioural therapy in the clinical management of tinnitus. *British Journal of Audiology, 22,* 265–272.

Marlatt, G. A., & Gordon, J. R. (1985). *Relapse prevention: Maintenance strategies in the treatment of addictive behaviors.* New York: Guilford Press.

Meichenbaum, D. H. (1975). Self instructional methods. In F. H. Kanfer & A. P. Goldstein (Eds.), *Helping people change: A textbook of methods.* New York: Pergamon Press.

Nezu, A. M., & Nezu, C. M. (1989). *Clinical decision making in behavior therapy: A problem-solving perspective.* Champaign, IL: Research Press.

Novaco, R. W. (1975*). Anger control: The development and evaluation of an experimental treatment.* Lexington, MA: Lexington.

Turk, D. C., Meichenbaum, D., & Genest, M. (1983). *Pain and behavioural medicine—A cognitive-behavioural perspective.* New York: Guilford Press.

Tyler, R. S. (Ed.). (2000). *Handbook of tinnitus.* San Diego: Singular Press.

Vernon, J. A. (Ed.). (1998). *Tinnitus: Treatment and relief.* Boston: Allyn and Bacon.

Vernon, J. A., & Moller, A. R. (Eds.). (1995). *Mechanisms of tinnitus.* Boston: Allyn and Bacon.

# *Appendix*

Tinnitus self-help associations exist in many countries. Listed below are several addresses for these associations.

American Tinnitus Association
P.O. Box 5
Portland, OR 97207-0005
Website address: www.ata.org

Australian Tinnitus Association
P.O. Box 660
Woollahra, NSW, 2025
Sydney, Australia
Website address:
   www.tinnitus.asn.au
Email: info@tinnitus.asn.au

British Tinnitus Association
14-18 West Bar Green
Sheffield, SA1 2DA
UK
Website address:
   www.tinnitus.org.uk
Email: comments@tinnitus.org.uk

Tinnitus Association of Canada
23 Ellis Park Road
Toronto, ON
M6S2V4
Canada

Website address: www.kadis.com/
   ta/tinnitus.htm
Email: chasm@pathcom.com

Federal Republic of Germany
Deutsche Tinnitus—Liga e.V (DTL)
Postfach 210351
42353 Wuppertal
Germany
Website address:
   www.tinnitus-liga.de
Email: dtl@tinnitus-liga.de

French Tinnitus Association
France Acouphenes
B.P. 547
75667 Paris Cedex 14
France
Website address: www.chez.com/
   acouphenes
Email:
   france.acouphenes@netcourier.
   com

# *Index*